Hold on to your Panties and have Fun

Hold on to your Panties and have Fun

Emily Joanne Hoover

authorHOUSE®

AuthorHouse™
1663 Liberty Drive
Bloomington, IN 47403
www.authorhouse.com
Phone: 1-800-839-8640

First published by AuthorHouse 10/20/2011

ISBN: 978-1-4670-2588-1 (sc)
ISBN: 978-1-4670-2590-4 (hc)
ISBN: 978-1-4670-2589-8 (ebk)

Library of Congress Control Number: 2011916045

Printed in the United States of America

This book is printed on acid-free paper.

Contents

Fun about This Book

If you are a prim and proper lady (and you know who you are), can't you find a book on history or religion? This book was written for "bad ass girls" of all ages. These are women who can sometimes get a little rowdy with their girlfriends (and you know who you are).

If you are an English major, you need to know I am a comic story teller. You can expect fun and funny life stories, not award winning wonderful.

If you are a man, what the Hell are you thinking? This book contains more delicate information that you can process. You are warned!

The rest of you hold on to your panties as you read interesting, inspiring and fun life stories that will have you LAUGHING OUT LOUD.

1

Fun Laughing Out Loud

This book doesn't contain anything perishable, liquid, or flammable. It does contain interesting, somewhat racy and shocking life stories that will have you LAUGHING OUT LOUD as you gain insight into your own life. In order to understand this book you may need to know how family and friends describe me. I was AMAZED at their answers.

"Funny" By a lot of people. Hey, better than funny looking.
"Outrageous" I try baby.
"Life of the party" Maybe.
"Potty Mouthed" You think?
"A hoot" By Ohio State University college roommates.
"A mess" By southern friends.
"A fat ass" By my brother when we were young.
"Bitch" You betcha!
"Strong Personality" That's better than weak, right?
"Amusing" Could it be?
"Beautiful" An old lady who can't see well. I told her she wasn't my type.
"Competitive" Showing my dogs. You betcha!
"Hot Lips" High school and college friends who tease me about playing the trumpet and the mellophone.
"Intelligent" Let's don't push that too far.

"Flaky" Does that mean fluffy like a wonderful southern biscuit?
"Charming" Seldom.
"Mischievous" You think?
"Endearing" You got to be kidding.
"Eccentric" One of a kind would be nicer doctor.
"Inspirational" Really?
"Pain in the ass" That's not surprising.
"Hot Foot" Isn't that what the fast lane is for? After all, being called "Hot Foot" and "Hot Lips" is the closest I have gotten to being called "A Hottie."
"Wild" By my Dalmatian pals. They probably know me best.
"Stylish" Hey, I try as long as it doesn't require pantyhose.
"A big mouth" O.k. I can't be good all the time. About 20 minutes is tops.
"Bossy" My mother. Who did she think I learned it from anyway?
"Obnoxious" O.k.! I can see where some who don't understand me could think that. And maybe some that do.
"Interesting" Hope so.
"Motivational" I try.
"Bad" I just try to make life around me as interesting and fun as possible. But yes, A LOT of people have said I am bad.

Some women might be horrified to be called bad. Since I am really good at being bad, I consider it an honor. Why? Read on.

2

Fun with Underwear

People seldom talk about underwear. I love to have fun with underwear. Maybe not the kind of fun you are thinking of. I have teased a couple of my long time guy (brother) friends about them being "boxer" or "brief" guys. Remember the TV ads? I like to have underwear fun with my girlfriends too! Question? Are you wearing your panties, or are you reading this commando?

I am at Walmart, my eye happens to catch sight of tiger print bikini panties. They were on sale for $3.00! Who of my many girlfriends could I have the most fun sending these to? Soon I am grinning thinking of my new adorable daughter-in-law and Viv, my 85 year old red-headed friend who acts 45, and is starting to date a younger guy. Both of these gals share my "wicked bad ass" sense of humor. I have to tell "the check out lady" of my plan to send these panties with a card that says, "Put a tiger in your tank girlfriend-grrr." Remember the TV ad for gas or cereal? She giggles and I laugh all the way home. I have to tell you that it's not often I crack myself up, but sometimes I can't help it.

I tell Hubby my plan and he grins. After putting my message on blank cards, I am soon on my way to the post office. The guy there recognizes me. He asks me if I have anything liquid, perishable, flammable, etc. I say, "No, they are just "tiger panties." His blush made my day! It takes so "little" to make me happy. The very next day I see Viv at bridge. She comes over, grinning and thanks me for the panties. I say, "What panties?" "You know damn well what panties. None of my other friends would do that!"

I say, "Really? What a pity," as I grin. She went on to say they "fit perfectly." I loved making her happy.

The other pair was sent to my daughter-in-law, and my son accidentally opened the envelope. Then he recognized my writing. Darn. She laughed and said she loved them.

Joni, one of my attractive Dal (Dalmatian) pals told me a funny story about traveling in Europe. She and a girlfriend had a flat tire on the German expressway. A "hunk" stopped to help them. As they opened the trunk there was all their underwear drying on a towel over their luggage. The hunk had a lot of fun teasing them and later sharing a beer. Isn't traveling fun?

My friend Judy S.—I know four Judy's—told me about her hard of hearing great grandma, at a funeral home drawing attention to herself by talking loudly. All of a sudden her panties fall off. What do you think she did? She simply bent over and pulled them up. <u>Sometimes you just gotta do what you gotta do</u>!

When I was growing up everyone had white cotton underwear. As a young child I had one piece with a drop down behind. I remember my younger sister being so excited about her brand new "day of the week" colored panties. Wondering, do you need to have a day of the week printed on your underwear to remember to change them every day? Did your mother ever tell you before you went ANYWHERE, "You need to have on clean underwear in case you are in an accident?" Let me tell you I have been in a bad accident and gone to the ER "several" times and NO ONE asked to see my underwear. <u>Almost</u> a disappointment after all that hype.

Years ago I was visiting my sister and her family. Her boys were fun loving pre-teens. My sister found my panties in the dryer. I put them in my handbag on the stairs because I didn't want the boys to find them and run around waving them.

Later that evening my sister and I went with her girl friends to dinner at a nice restaurant, when I opened my bag to pay for dinner I found my panties. My sister and I giggled. Her friends wanted to know what was so funny. So I showed them and my sister explained how the panties got in there. She says they still talk about it.

Is it the English that say, "Don't get your knickers or britches in a bunch." Southerners say, "Don't get your panties in a wad." Don't both mean, don't get upset over nothing?

Maybe you've heard, "Put on your big girl panties and deal with it." I say, "HOLD ON TO YOUR PANTIES AND HAVE FUN!"

3

Fun with Doctors

Before I went to Ohio State I never used bad four-letter words or gave doctors a rough time. Menopause is to blame. I sort of lost interest in sex and gained a whole new appreciation for all kinds of humor.

I do love to surprise, and yes, yes, yes—I love to embarrass "the big guys" who take life so seriously! Maybe it was—could easily have been—my three or four "near-death" experiences that made me look for fun. I've reached that age where I have to deal with doctors more often. Frankly, those experiences are just NOT fun! Thus, damn it, I'm going to make them fun—somehow.

Dr. Feelgood is very bright. His staff had kept me waiting in his office a long time. I was trapped in a small room with no magazines. All there was to do was stare at his bulletin board of family snapshots. When the doctor came in, I commented on how attractive his wife was and I went on to say how lucky he was. He thanked me. I said, "Can't quite figure it out." He remained silent. I added, "Since she obviously didn't marry you for your looks, you must have been good in bed." While keeping his gaze on my medical chart, the embarrassed doctor said, "I'll have you know we didn't have sex before marriage." I said, "Way to go, neither did we," and patted him on the shoulder. I still can't believe I said that. He quickly got on with my case.

During the next visit he was discussing giving me a cortisone shot in my knee. He said, "Anytime you put a needle in, you run the risk of infection and then you could DIE." Exact words—I swear. I said, "Let's go for it. Sometimes I live on the edge." After the shot he said, "You stay here—I'll have the nurse check on you." I said, "So you want me to die right here?" He called back, "Better here than the parking lot." I think he's getting the hang of handling "Every Doctor's Worst Nightmare"—me.

Locally, we have a hunky and well-respected surgeon, Dr. Orthro. He writes a weekly column in our little newspaper. He had written about research showing that chewing gum will relieve gas after abdominal surgery. He went on to say: ". . . although passing gas in a social situation isn't desirable, in a hospital it can be cherished." Can you believe "cherished"? So when I met him I said, "I wanted to meet the doctor who said farts are to be cherished." Dr. Ortho got red and grinned. "You are just the cutest thing when you blush," I said. Even Hubby was amused.

Giving doctors a rough time is so easy for me, and what fun! I have found that they WILL remember you from all the hundreds of other patients they see. Several of the nurses have told me that I made their doctor's day.

When my first ovarian tumor burst, Hubby took me to our small hospital. Dr. Learning Intern, was on duty. He did X-rays etc. and—even a pregnancy test. Finally, after three or four hours, he told me, "We can't find anything wrong with you, except your intestines are quite full." I said, "Are you trying to tell me that I'm just full of shit?" My GYN, who was head of staff, enjoyed hearing the story.

Later I developed another tumor, cancer grade 1. If it had burst, I wouldn't be here. So I had a spay job. (I know it's a hysterectomy.)

In the hospital after two or three days of nothing but plain Jell-O, plain broth, and apple juice, I needed real food. I decided to go "on strike"! "You can leave the apple juice, but I don't want the broth or jello." The shocked pink lady said, "You don't want it?" I said sweetly, "No, I want real food." She told me that this was what my doctor ordered. I said, "He doesn't have to eat it. When she came back she said, surprised, "You didn't eat your Jell-O or your broth." Patiently, I said, "No, I'm on strike."

Another nurse tried later to get me to have some broth and Jell-O. I repeated: "Sorry, I'm on strike." The next morning they sent in the nurse from Hell (maybe a former sergeant in the Army) trying to get me to eat.

I said, "Couldn't you find me a piece of toast?" She returned with toast. Oh, I enjoyed it! Real food!

In about 15 minutes the pain began—WOW, what gas pains!!!! Sergeant-nurse came in and asked me if I had gas pain. I said sweetly, "A little." She then became a real sweetie and offered to wash out her cup and heat up some apple juice, saying it would help. I told her I was fine even though I thought I was dying. The pain went away almost immediately after I drank the hot juice. From then on I could eat regular food.

A day later she said, "The doctor wants you walking. Why don't you come down to see the twins?" Frankly, I think babies are like parasites. They are all about "me-me-me," aren't they? They usually aren't cute unless they are yours, right? I wanted to get out of the hospital ASAP, so I went down to the viewing window to see the babies. They were about 14 inches in length, with big, square heads and lots of black hair. Not attractive, but I guess not super ugly either. The nurse asked me what I thought. "I'm just glad I had a tumor," I said.

During my checkup I asked the doctor if he'd heard about my "strike." "Of course," as he grinned.

When my OBGYN retired, my Dalmatian pal, Diana, recommended Dr. Spread Yours. He was from Clearwater, Florida, and we both knew some of the same families. When he asked how I felt, I said "Fine for an old bitch." The nurse told me they'd had a rough day and that I made their day.

At the next visit, his nurse told me she was expecting fun. So when the doctor came in I said, "We want to know what you recommend in vibrators." He was forty something, blushed and said he didn't know and added, "I know what you DON'T want." Together we asked, "What?" "The ones with the very small lead balls, as they have been known to get lost in the vagina." We looked at one another. I said, "I guess we don't want those, do we?" She laughed and shook her head "no." (Barbara was about 35, cute, and single.)

Then I asked him if he watched *Sex and the City*. He said "Not anymore—after the blonde became so promiscuous." I said, "Doc, get real, most young girls are like that today!" she nodded her head. Then, line for line, I told him about Suzanne and the vibrator show. It was well-written—funny and, yes, shocking! I laughed out loud as the doctor's face turned red. He said, "Let's get on with the exam."

While he was looking in there, I said in a loud voice, "For women everywhere, we HATE, HATE, HATE this!" He said, "We guys have to go through a similar thing." "Yeah sure, a little touchy-touchy, feely-feely, and a cough. Nowhere near as uncomfortable or invasive as what women go through." After he had finished, I said, "But I would rather be a woman than a man." He seemed surprised. "You would?" I said, "Yes, I would rather have something between my ears than something between my legs." Barbara thought that was funny. My Dalmatian friend, Lucy, says I was definitely "the crotch-du-jour patient of the week."

When it was time for my next appointment, I was so embarrassed I considered finding a new doctor. Sometimes God is busy elsewhere. After much thought, I decided to take my doctor a present of homemade North Carolina apple butter. (No, baby, I didn't make it. Is my name Martha?) Dr. Spread Yours always seemed happy to see me. Sometimes the worse you are to a guy, the more he likes you.

I asked Dr. Spread Yours to recommend a good heart doctor for my husband. In fact, Dr. Spread Yours had his mom fly up to Atlanta to go to Dr. Heart. He is one of only a few doctors in the world to do a heart operation that leaves only a three-inch scar. My Hubby had a prolapsed valve and was to have surgery.

I met Dr. Heart shortly after 9/11 and I asked him to please save my Hubby's life, not just for me, but for our country. I told him Hubby had over a dozen patents. Sometimes it's good for doctors to know there are other very bright people.

Hubby was back to work full time is less than three weeks. At his final check-up, the nurse told him to leave his shirt off as Dr. Heart wanted to take a photo. After the exam Dr. Heart went to get his camera. (Question: With what he makes wouldn't you think they'd have a camera in each office?) When he came back, I said, "Does Hubby own the rights to these pictures?" Hubby was concerned as he saw the twinkle of mischief coming. The doctor said, "No, I use these photos to teach other doctors throughout the world."

Talk about modest. I think, *OK, big guy, time for" this mama" to bring you back to the real world.* When the doctor stopped at the center island to write a few notes, I put my arm around him and whispered loudly in his ear, "Thank you so much, for saving my Hubby's life. But while you were in there, couldn't you have worked on something farther down that could work better?" As his nurse's laughter almost drowned out his answer, he blushed and said, "Well, he should breathe better now."

Lordy, Lordy, Lordy, I hope I don't have to ask Dr. Heart to save *my* life someday. God, let me get by with "being bad" again. Thank you, God. It made my day—week—month—maybe year. Could I be a Doctor's Worst Nightmare?

4

Fun in Small Towns

Don't you just love small towns? I do! I was born about a mile from Martinsville, Ohio. This very small town is located in southern Ohio, midway between Cincinnati and Columbus. I was born in 1935 at my paternal grandparents' home. Surprising for those times, a female physician delivered me. My mother had twilight sleep, one of the first childbirth pain drugs.

Hubby and I call two small towns home. We spend eight months in Florida on a small island, we call Paradise. It is covered with lush oaks, palms, azaleas, oleander and colorful plants. The curving roads reach from the sandy beach to the quiet, small town. Shops stock all kinds of goodies for us and the ever-arriving tourists. It is a small place where not everyone knows our name, but often we run into people who do.

A few years ago, Faye loaned us her North Carolina house for a weekend. We fell in love with the mountains and the cooler summer temperatures. We bought a small home with a lovely view close to town. Faye holds the title of my "most expensive" friend.

Occasionally I get into way too much fun/trouble in our small towns. Often, I think out loud, or act before I think. I will do almost anything to get a laugh.

Faye and I were at a restaurant on the beach. We said "Hi!" to mutual friends. Soon we noticed the owner of another local restaurant come in; I sort of knew him. He and his party sat at a table nearby. We smiled. Soon it became apparent they were celebrating his big "5-0" birthday.

As his large cake arrived, his party started singing "Happy Birthday." I encouraged other people to join in. With a flushed face, the guy stood to cut the cake. His girlfriend gave him a kiss. Bad girl that I am, I walked over and planted one on him too. His friends loved it (him not so much). He blushed. (Yeah, yeah, yeah!) You won't believe what happened next. He offered Faye and me some cake. Was that neat or not?

One day I had a lot of things on my mind. I was outside Walmart and gave the Veterans all my change since I was out of folding money. Then I stopped at a restaurant for their delicious tomato bisque soup. I grabbed for my handbag only to discover it missing. I went into panic mode BIG TIME!

I rapidly reversed and arrived back at Walmart as I was praying really hard. "God, please help me. You know I just gave all my money to a worthy cause. God, that ought to count for something."

My bag held a few charge cards, my driver's license, insurance cards, checkbook, and cell phone. I kept praying on my way to the customer service desk.

"Has anyone turned in a grey metallic handbag?"

Lucky for me, the lady wasn't busy. She held up my bag and said, "Is this yours?"

I gave her a hug and, with tears in my eyes, I said, "Yes, thank you and thank God you have it."

"Who turned it in?" I asked, as I found nothing missing. She said, "A middle-aged guy."

She said, "That's him going out the door." I ran after him, yelling, "Hey, Mister!" He stopped.

I said, "Thank you so much for turning in my bag," and I hugged him. I asked him if I could offer him a reward. He said, "No, but if you need a DJ sometime, keep me in mind," as he handed me his business card and told me about his regular Wednesday night gig.

One evening I stopped by where he was working for a burger. I chatted with him and found out the name of his favorite restaurant. Later after discussing doing right in life and God I took him a gift card with the book, The Game of Life and How to Play It by Florence Scovel Shinn. What a sweet nice guy!

Taco Bell saved my life—so to speak. Can you imagine life without pizza, spaghetti, or burgers? I had skin tests done and found out I am allergic to wheat. I now can have small amounts of whole wheat.

At the drive-thru, I ordered two hard tacos, onions and hot sauce.

A young voice asked me if I wanted "hot or mild sauce."

I said, "Hot, as I am a hot mama," and laughed.

When I arrived at the window I said, "I bet you thought I was a lot younger and a lot hotter."

We laughed again.

What fun! Love, love, love having fun with people of all ages! The possibilities are endless!

A few years ago on April 1st, I was in our local health food store. One of the guys had been playing April Fools' jokes on everyone. He told me when the owner came in, he was going to inform him his son needed money and to be picked up at the tattoo shop.

When he went to get me something, a gal told me, "I have been trying to get him all day."

I said, "I can do that, no problem."

When he returned and rang up my purchase, I leaned over and whispered, "As soon as you finish, you might want to go in the restroom and check the back of your pants."

A worried look came over his face, as he turned one way and the other looking over his shoulder. I said, "April Fool! Got you!" We all laughed. Him? Not so much.

Did I feel guilty? No, as he had been having the same kind of fun all day. We still laugh about it.

I can get you even if you don't know me. Hubby and I had gone to a family restaurant for lunch. We were surprised to see three middle-aged guys picking up a lot of balloons. Did they fall out of the sky?

Bad girl that I am, I said, "I hope none of you guys are going to use them for condoms."

One said, "No, Ma'am."

I need to tell you Hubby gave me one of those "How could you" looks, but followed it with a grin. (I say the "look" doesn't count if you grin either before or after.)

At the grocery store, I stood behind a woman who had twelve bottles of wine in her grocery cart. When our eyes met, I said, "Looks like you're going to have a real party or a real headache."

She laughed and said, "That's good."

One day Hubby and I were at Lowe's. While in line I got to chatting with a real cute couple. She was "very pregnant." In their cart were some short white flowers.

I asked if I could look at the information tag.

The man said, "Sure, we bought the same kind last year and they bloomed all summer."

I said, "I don't think these are for me since they are annuals."

His wife said, "Ours came back and are blooming again."

I said, "Really."

"Maybe I got lucky," the husband said.

I looked at his wife and said, "Looks like it—at least once with her and once with the plants."

They laughed.

Hubby sometimes doesn't appreciate the fun as much as I. You can laugh at me, with me, or frown. I might be the cause of his forehead wrinkles, though. He has awesome wrinkles running horizontally as well as vertically. If he would take a nap and sleep on his back, I could play miniature checkers on his forehead. Could I be the cause of his wrinkles? You betcha. And do I feel guilty? Not often!

5

Fun with Family

Not everyone could take a mother like me. Our two sons, who like their mother both have been real challenges at times, have turned out to be truly neat people.

Most people think S.C., our first, is very handsome and looks like me. Guess I should have been a man. I remember his kindergarten teacher and I wanted to hold him back. His dad said he needed to be in first grade. I should have protested. Although super bright, he was socially immature and had trouble taking directions maybe like his mom. I tutored him between third and fourth grade. He was a very bright, but stubborn kid who didn't want to learn his multiplication tables. I bought a phonograph record that taught multiplication, and told him that he could learn them and spend the rest of his summer reading and playing, or I would tutor him every summer forever. Dumb, he was not! He got the point! He still cringes when I sing the multiplication song.

He was still goofing around in high school. Had I thought of it, I would have taken off work and gone to school and sat in on his classes all day long. Once would have been enough.

As a teenager he turned over his Dad's car going too fast on gravel and totaled mine. He moved on to a motorcycle. He has had nine motorcycle or car accidents—that I know of. The last time, he broke his arm, I took him to the doctor. I told S.C. I wasn't going to do it anymore. Thank God I haven't had to.

S.C. has a wicked dry humor, much like his dad's. He is a self-educated mechanical engineer (Yeah for math records). He has two patents and a published paper. As a child, he always loved taking things apart to see what made them work. In high school, he was happy when we let him have my dead Fiat to work on. He was always hitting me up for cash for parts. I gave in during "the lean years" to help him stay out of the usual teenage trouble.

Once, when he was about 11 we were eating dinner and discussing the planned breeding of our first Champion Dalmatian.

I said, "Can you believe I was the only one in my family that was planned?"

Quick on the draw, S.C. said, "Gee, Mom, to look at you, no one would believe you were planned."

We not only love him, but are very proud of S.C. He has made a lot of difficult decisions. Going through a painful divorce, dating, and starting a business during trying times isn't easy. About a year ago he married a wonderful woman. They seem to complement each other. She is bright, attractive, fun, and a successful business owner. He is one lucky guy. We love them both.

I must mention he can drive me crazy. S.C. decided to take a week long motorcycle trip alone from near Savannah, out to the Pacific Northwest, camping most of the way. Boy, did I pray . . . a LOT. Think about those nine accidents he had. Thank You, God, for getting him home safely. If he weren't so sweet at times, I might want to give him away.

T.J., our youngest, was always quiet as a child, yet is completely the opposite now. He surprised us when he was 10 with his first successful newspaper sales job. He did better in school than S.C., but he too should have been held back. As a former teacher, I think all boys should be seven before first grade. I wish I had fought to do this with ours.

T.J., as a young teen, had the neatest dreams of European travel and they have all come true! After high school T.J. was an exchange student in Finland for several months. When he came home he decided to join the Air Force, to travel and obtain his education. He worked 40-hour weeks as a history writer at Marsh Air Force Base in Southern California. He earned his B.A. degree in business and a Master's in education during this time. However, after seven years and a tour of Iceland, he left the service.

T.J. had multiple challenges, having married too young, having a child, and then being divorced. He recently completed his Masters in divinity.

We were not allowed to see our only grandchild, J.D., until he was about two. When he was seven he was able to have a visit for a week. People said he looked like his dad T.J. at the same age. They also said T.J. and J.D. have my sense of mischief. Both like to travel. T.J. had a successful real estate career. He "came out" many years ago and has been with his partner for almost 25 years. We all love and appreciate his partner, R.R. Many of my friends and people at his church have told me how much they admire and like him. T.J. is very outgoing and very successful at developing and promoting his Church outreach programs. I know he will be a wonderful minister.

T.J. and I have a sort of humorous competition thing. He or I will call each other and say, "You won't believe what mischief I got into." A few years ago when he and R.R. lived on our Island they used the same small bank I did. The three tellers knew he was my son. When I went through the drive-in, they asked me how I was. I said, "Fine, for an old bitch." They loved it! If I just said, "Great!" they'd look disappointed. T.J. went through the drive-in and they asked him how he was. Guess what he said? That bad boy said, "Fine, for a son of a bitch." I guess one teller almost wet her panties. He has <u>almost</u> as much fun in life as I do.

There's no doubt about it, J.D. is my FAVORITE GRANDCHILD. I know I shouldn't say that, but he turns out to be my only grandchild. Now in his mid-20s, he has gone through some rough times in his life. J.D.'s mom died at 42. I loved her.

When J.D. was about 17 he lived with T.J. full-time. A few years earlier, I was in Texas visiting and helping T.J. at work and visiting with the guys. T.J. asked me to take J.D. out for practice driving. (I had taught T.J. how to drive.) I said I would. Well, after a while J.D. stopped the car and asked me to drive. Apparently I didn't have enough patience when I was sitting in the "death seat." J.D. took more classes.

Since he was working, T.J. asked me to take my grandson for his driving test. It was raining. When I picked him up afterwards he was frowning. I said, "What's wrong? You didn't have an accident, did you?" Turns out he had, when turning left in his instructor's truck. Not fun for him or his family—definitely not for his instructor.

His dad didn't want him driving in "crazy Texas metro traffic," going to school events, work, etc. After much discussion, it was decided that an international school in Italy would be an enriching experience. As a young child, J.D. has always loved to draw. He drew whenever he had an opportunity. He has a God-given talent. In Italy his art teacher encouraged him and helped sell $300 of his art. I would think most teenage boys would buy electronic toys or CDs, but J.D. bought a white suit, a marine-blue shirt, and a silver tie. (No, he isn't gay.) He likes to dress nicely. He purchased the suit to wear to his senior dance, graduation, and on our cruise after graduation.

About the time J.D. graduated, the guys moved to Paradise Island. After high school graduation J.D. came home, went to college, and worked part-time. Life was not easy for him and his dad. J.D. had reached "I know more than you do, Dad" stage. Soon he joined the Air Force. After three years service J.D. got out and moved in with us. We got along very well. I stayed up until he'd get home after midnight. I wanted to be there for him. We usually talked for an hour or more. Even though I wasn't part of his early life, we have always been close. He is so funny, so sweet, and so much fun. Do I spoil him? Maybe a little.

About that time I decided I needed some part-time household help. A bridge friend had recommended Dagmar. She attended college and did a cleaning job part-time. J.D. wanted to know, after I talked with her, if she was a HOTTIE.

I said, "I just talked to her on the phone."

He said, "But did she sound hot?"

I said, "How would I know?"

The day she came, I was in the back of the house. Our dog, Tex, barked, and J.D. got out of bed and told me that Dagmar was at the door. He returned to his room to dress.

I opened the door and said loudly, "Hey J.D., she is a hottie!" before I even said "hi" to her.

How did our family begin? My husband and I met on a blind date at Ohio State. We both worked our way through college, so we were not able to attend football games regularly. (We did meet Archie Griffin who is a twice-Heisman trophy winner.) When I went to the games it was to see and hear the Ohio State Marching Band. It was, and perhaps still is, the only band of its type, comprised primarily of brass and drums. I was so disappointed in 1954 that I couldn't try out as it was an all male band. Thank God they got over that!

I've always been attracted to very intelligent men, especially engineers. I grew up in the era of "no sex before marriage," which was not easy. I fell in love with my guy's adorable grin, intelligence, twinkling eyes, dry wit, and work ethic. I loved that he was such a gentleman. He is extremely quiet, serious, loves the outdoors, walking, camping, swimming, hiking, and canoeing. I think the outdoors is for viewing, painting, art, parades, and dog shows. He likes orchestras. I love bands of all types: Dixieland, jazz, concert, and marching. He loves operas as much as I dislike them. He likes to be with one or two couples at a time. I love parties, especially BIG ones. He would rather listen to music and read (which I like as well), but I do love parties: even though I am a one-or two-drink gal.

Hubby is quite an asset to his company. He has over a dozen patents as well as published papers. The much younger PhDs tell me they are all trying to learn as much as they can from him before he finally leaves the workforce. Sometimes it seems my dog talks to me more than he does. We have gone through a lot of difficulties in our marriage, but we are always there for one another. We are both forgiving. We love, trust, and respect one another. I "kid" Hubby that after over 50 years of marriage I would like a great-looking 50-year-old. Ha-ha! Fat chance of that happening. At times Hubby is much too serious for me, and sometimes I'm too wild for him. We get over it. We do enjoy being quiet together, reading, watching TV, or walking on the beach. I think our relationship works because I see him as "my quiet and steady rock" and I bring smiles to his face for some (NOT ALL) of my actions. We each like our "alone time."

Hubby is so focused when he's working on anything. He is a nicer and better person than I am. I wish I could be more like him. Believe it or not, we rarely argue, though it does take a conversation to do that. Rather than hearing ugly words, I see the facial disapproval. Do you think this is how he got all those wrinkles?

I love that Hubby has always been kind towards my friends, relatives, and my dogs. He is a good guy, especially to put up with me.

When S.C. was about 16, I overheard him say to his dad, "Sometimes I don't know what you see in Mom."

(Of course I eavesdropped.)

He said, "Your mother is a very exciting woman. I never know quite what she is going to do."

I'll do just about anything to see that adorable grin of his.

6

Fun with Voodoo Doctors

Voodoo—you know I'm kidding. You may not be as open to alternative health care as I.

I believe in vitamins and herbs that I get at health food stores. I have found the people there to be very helpful, as well as a lot of fun.

In North Carolina, the health food store owners used to be married to each other. They still get along great. I asked the guy why they got divorced. (Hey, inquiring people want to know.) He said he was immature. They've been divorced for several years.

Last year she married someone else. My friend told me that he liked the new husband. Six months later they both were at the checkout counter when I asked her, "How's the new marriage going?" She grins and says, "Really good." I say as I look him in the eye, "Anything is an improvement, right?" They both laugh.

Moving around the country or having back problems while out of town, I have been to a lot of different chiropractors. All helped me, thank God. I have been to two sets of married chiropractors. Often I tease the wife by saying, "I need your husband's hot hands upon my body." Their laughter makes my day.

My current chiropractor I call Dr. Hottie. One Valentine's Day when I saw him, I asked, if he was going to get lucky that evening? I know I shouldn't do this, but I just can't help myself. He was speechless and he grinned. He always has a big smile for me as he gives me a hug.

Recently I told his wife that I had given him a rough time. She said, "Good, he needs it." I also told her that I had said, "If I have to have a doctor's hands on my body, I want him to look hot." She says, "Now there will be no living with him."

Another chiropractor I used to go to was celebrating his 45th birthday. I told a sweet lady in the waiting room, "Doctor is celebrating his 50th birthday." "Really he looks more like forty." I said, "Why don't you tell him he doesn't look 50?" Of course she did. When she comes out with the "grinning doctor," she pokes her finger in my face and says, "Thanks to you, I can't come back here again." I pat her on the shoulder and say, "I'm so sorry." The doctor laughed. What a good sport!

Acupuncture has been around for over 5,000 years. It wouldn't have lasted if it didn't help people? I believe the combo of chiropractic and acupuncture keeps me going since I was born with curvature of the spine. The acupuncture needles are as fine as a piece of hair so it doesn't hurt. It is NOT like a shot. One acupuncturist from China told me that every medical doctor in China had to be certified in acupuncture before medical school. He calls me Maxi needles.

I would urge anyone to try acupuncture several times before joint or back surgery. So far it has worked for me.

Unfortunately, so far, acupuncturist services are not usually covered by insurance. Some doctors do have deals on a set of treatments. An acupuncturist helped me get over a horrible cold while on my cruise with J.D. She told me that frequently U.S. medical doctors will try acupuncture on a cruise ship. She treated a surgeon for shoulder problems. He was so impressed he decided to add an acupuncturist to his new clinic. Too bad they have to get out of our country to try it.

To find a good chiropractor or acupuncturist, look for experience and ask for recommendations.

7

Fun with Animals

I have always loved animals, especially dogs. My mother bought a Scottish terrier when I was young and gave it away when it had fleas. Today we have flea control, but in the '30s and '40s there wasn't such a thing. A lovely red Irish setter appeared at our home when I was six. How I loved "Red." It broke my heart when my dad found the owner. A year later Mother ordered—I believe, from a Sears or J. C. Penney catalog—a Saint Bernard. Fortunately, the family decided to keep the puppy as I doubt that my mother could have coped with such a large breed.

When I was starting 3rd grade, during World War II, my dad gave up being a supervisor for the CCC (Civilian Conservation Corps, Roosevelt's program for building roads, bridges, etc.). We moved to Dad's parents' farm. My sister, Dawn, says it was because we were having trouble getting food. I always thought it was because my grandfather was getting older and needed manpower, since all available able-bodied men had joined the Army. Our Dad had medical disabilities—able to work, but unable to serve.

My brother, sister, and I rode the bus to school and often walked the mile back. One day a dog followed us home, no doubt encouraged by us kids. My dad called her "Pooch." Mother renamed her. We called her "Poochee"—adding a French twist. How I loved her.

I was a sophomore in college when "Poochee" died. My dad, who had a wonderful way with words, wrote me a beautiful letter. He told me she had wandered away one day, never to be seen again. I wonder. In those days you didn't call someone; you wrote letters. My dad was an honest guy, but not above "protecting me." I carried that letter with me and was very upset when I lost it.

When I was 11, Aunt Emily and Uncle Carl bought a Dalmatian for their daughter, Ada Marie. "Roxie," was the most beautiful dog I had ever seen. I loved how regal she was and how beautifully she moved.

When our oldest son, S.C. was two, I started wanting a dog for him. He adored a neighbor's buff cocker. We bought a black and tan AKC dachshund. Hubby built her the cutest red pagoda-type roof dog house with open sides. For short periods of time, we put her on a long chain attached to the corner of the dog house. Most of the time she was in our house. I was teaching so I hired a babysitter for S.C. All went well for several months, and then the dog started getting nasty. She had jumped up on a dining room chair, to the table, and was having her second dinner, while I took S.C. to the bathroom. When I scolded her, she bared her teeth. I grabbed her by the collar and removed her. She chewed on S.C.'s expensive wooden toys. Later I found out this is normal for doxies. After she snapped at Hubby and the babysitter, that was it! We gave her to a couple who lived one street over. All went well until they had a baby. I guess that dachshund didn't have patience with little ones.

When we moved to Clearwater we acquired "Tom Cat," a plain, yellow-striped cat. The boys loved him. He was an outside cat during the day and in the garage at night. He loved to climb up on our tile roof and position himself perfectly over the center of the front door.

A few weeks later he fell through the screened ceiling of our neighbors' porch while chasing their bird. Needless to say, that didn't go over well. We replaced the screening. It was upsetting for them and us. I couldn't keep him in the house due to allergies. "Tom Cat" went to live in a barn on a farm.

Soon we moved into a townhouse in Santa Clara, California. Along came a kid selling a puppy for "only" five dollars. "Beau" was part sheepdog and part Border collie. The boys (3 and 6) were mildly interested in him. I have no use for barking dogs. (Later I found out barking is not uncommon in herding breeds.) The babysitter would put him on the patio. After awhile he'd bark and she'd let him in. Thus he learned to bark for attention. Pollen on his coat became a big problem for me. He went to a farm and was trained to herd cattle. Thank God!

When we moved into a house in Los Altos, California, Hubby decided to get the boys some baby ducks. The subdivision had been an apricot orchard. When the apricots started falling, the ducks got diarrhea, big time. We survived. Then one fall night we heard a lot of quacking. Apparently a fox had killed a couple of ducks. The next day Hubby took the others to a park with a pond. The boys missed them; I didn't!

I was done with pets! I was teaching full-time, had a busy family life and community activities. I really don't know how I did it all. I was taking classes towards my master's; I was in American Association of University Women, Junior Woman's Club, and on the Board for Missionaries at our Methodist church. It helped that I was usually home by four o'clock and took advantage of planning periods. We had a neighborhood teen come in to run the vacuum and help fold clothes. I DID NOT NEED OR WANT ANY MORE PETS—EVER!

To find out how did I go from wanting NO pets to being Dalmatian obsessed, read on.

8

Fun with Spotted Fever

No sooner had our pet ducks gone to live at the park lake than my boys started talking about getting a dog. I said, "No more dogs!" After several weeks I was outvoted. Hubby started by saying, "Every boy needs a dog." S.C., our oldest son, was into watching *Lassie* and wanted a collie. I said, "No long-haired dogs. If we get a dog it has to be a Dalmatian." A litter was advertised in the local newspaper and I have had chronic Spotted Fever since 1966.

We fell in love with a lightly hand-painted, beautiful black-and-white little girl with blue eyes. On the way home we stopped at the vet for her shots. She was in excellent health. Hubby built a really nice pen for her in the garage. The boys played with her in the backyard and she spent quality time in the house. She was adorable!

After a few weeks I mentioned to the art teacher I taught with, that it was strange the puppy would not wake up when I opened the garage door. He said maybe she was deaf. I found out it can happen in Dalmatians.

None of the books I had read mentioned deafness. She was deaf. Heartbreaking! The puppy was returned and we found a champion-sired lovely litter.

They were three weeks old and oh so cute. Their mama was sweet with them and us. At six weeks we took our "Ladybug" home. We agreed to show her. She was a sweetheart and the boys loved her.

Little did I know this action would lead me on an over forty-year involvement, love, and obsession with the breed. I was hooked at the first match, when Ladybug got a blue ribbon. Soon we went to the San Francisco Cow Palace to see American/Canadian Champion Pacifica Pride of Poseidon, Ladybugs sire, and a lot of his kids in a big show. Sy took Best of Breed. He was a flashy marked black-and-white, very showy, sweet dog. We also saw some of his liver-and-white (brown-and-white) kids. Six months later we moved near Atlanta, Georgia, and began taking Ladybug to show class. She was a real challenge, not wanting to stand still or have her toenails done.

We kept in touch with Sy's owner, as promised. Soon, Sy received his Best in Show. Unfortunately, Ladybug was disqualified as a "patch" at her first big show. A patch is a genetic defect—a large area of color present at birth. Normally, Dalmatians are white at birth and start getting the spots at ten days old. She was not reinstated since some of the judges didn't know that spots can grow together, but if white hairs are present it is "not" a patch.

I still wanted to show Dalmatians. Thus we got another sweet Sy puppy, who later became our first Champion, Atlantis Love of Pacifica. A year later Fred sent us Love's mom, Lady of Carpenterdal (show quality) bred to Poseidon. She was due to have puppies in two weeks. She was a very loving girl and easy to live with. All that had come from the Pacifica line have been loving, sweet, adorable, and so much fun. They are like a really good chocolate chip cookie—one seldom is enough!

The boys and Hubby seemed to love them as much as I. Two years later we had five and a litter on the way. We started looking for more space, a Dalmatian plantation. All our neighbors liked our dogs and told us they didn't want us to move. We soon found what we thought was our dream country home on eight acres.

Hubby and I became founding members of the Dalmatian Club of Greater Atlanta. Later I would also become a founding member of the Mid-Florida Dalmatian Club. Our Atlantis Dalmatians were written up in a book published in Spain. They were also written up in The New Dalmatians: Coach Dog: Firehouse Dog written by Esmeralda and Alfred Treen, published by Howell Books in 1980, long considered the Bible on Dalmatians.

Spotted Fever anyone?

9

Fun and Sewer Magic

Have you ever met anyone who fell into a septic tank? Kinda sh***y. It happened to Johnny, one of my "houseboys" (the guys who help build or maintain our house and yard). He apparently walked on the top cover, it split, and he fell in, fortunately only to the knees. It could have been worse—yucky, yucky, yucky, gross, gross, and really gross. He worked for a septic tank cleaning business before he got into yard work. I wonder what attracts people to do really yucky jobs, don't you?

I told Johnny my own septic tank story. We purchased an eight-acre property in Roswell, Georgia, to have room for our Dalmatians. During the more than 35 years we lived there, we always called the same septic tank company. The owner and sometimes his dad would come to clean it out. We knew we needed their help when water wouldn't drain properly from the downstairs shower.

Helen, Dalmatian pal, and Linda, another Dal pal, had come to visit and told us about the slow draining shower. Don't catastrophes always happen when you have company? The upstairs bath also ran to the septic tank, so it had to be fixed, even though we had recently sold our property. The house would be moved. We hated to spend more money. However, we had no choice. I called our longtime septic company.

A new employee cleaned it, but still we had a problem. He called the owner, and then told me his boss would be out to investigate the situation.

A woman I kind of remembered seeing, showed up. She told me she was following her grandfather and father in the business. Always for women's rights, I told her I was proud of her owning her own business.

She was something else: about 5'5", a pretty face, with long, dark curly hair. She had a big smile, bigger shoulders, large arms, and stomach. She wore a shirt tucked into her too-tight jeans, with her belt under her stomach. From the rear she looked like a short plump guy.

She inspected our septic tank and checked the bathroom. Then she told me she had to go home to get her video camera.

I said, "Beg your pardon?"

She said, "I have a video camera that I can snake down this toilet to check out your lines to see where the problem is."

When she was back, I just had to watch. I've got to tell you, this magic made my day. How many of you have looked into your drains through a video camera? She found a crack with a plant growing into it. This had caused the drainage to back up.

My septic tank expert had brought along her well-behaved, pretty five-year-old daughter. She told me she hoped her daughter would grow up to take over the family business . . . every little girl's dream. Maybe instead of a Barbie Doll her mother's Christmas gift was a toy septic truck and a miniature septic tank.

About that time, Lucy, my Dal pal of over 40 years, called. When I told her about all this, she recounted another true story. Her brother came to visit her at her old farmhouse. The septic tank was located on the bathroom side of the house. A grease trap ran from the kitchen. As best I can remember, a grease trap is basically a pipe from the kitchen that leads away from the house and drains the dishwater. Sometimes it could be quite damp and mushy. Her brother walked into the grease trap and sank down to his ankles. Lucy tried to warn him but could only say "Oh no!" when she realized it was too late. He jokingly told her, "I'm going to sewer you."

Lucy also told me her Alabama septic tank company was family-owned. Their name being Rose.

I replied, "Do they have a sign on their truck that reads 'We leave your place smelling like a rose'?"

Someone recently told me about a local septic company. They guarantee their services or double your load back.

I told this story to a bridge buddy gal pal, Babs, and she told me she once dropped her keys in a urinal.

"How did that happen?" I asked.

"Well, you know how port-a-potties always have urinals. I was using the toilet, but I accidently dropped my keys in the urinal. Fortunately my boyfriend fished them out for me."

I said, "Reminds me of one of my gross experiences. After I had tinkled, my wallet slid off the toilet into the gross gas station toilet." Yucky, yucky, yucky, gross, gross, and more gross! I had to get it out, and washed and dried it best I could. I replaced my wallet ASAP. However, I understand that urine disinfects, but I didn't know that at the time.

Don't I have an interesting life?

10

Fun with the Girls

"You are so bad!" said Becky, a friend from the Newcomers Club. We played bridge together, and were past members of a Red Hat's group. We decided they were lovely ladies, but maybe too nice for us.

I try to keep healthy, so I joined Curves. Curves has been a challenge, however I like the people, and exercise helps me feel better. I lost thirty pounds the first year. Then I joined TOPS (Take Off Pounds Sensibly) to force myself to be accountable. There are great gals who have been very supportive of my book, in both of those groups.

Growing up I liked playing softball and basketball. For years, I used to keep my weight down by showing my Dalmatians.

Why show dogs? It's exercise, travel, plus you can joke around with friends and play with your dogs. A big plus is that it gets you out of the kitchen!

Cathy is one of my long time friends, who no longer show Dalmatians. My favorite Cathy story is about our trip to Las Vegas (probably close to 12 years ago). Years ago I worked for Cathy in her decorating business. She and I often stayed at each other's home. We both love decorating, Dalmatians, fashion, and share our special Lhasa friend, Patti. We always have a fun time.

While visiting Cathy she told me about going to a bridal show in Las Vegas. I told her Hubby never wanted to go. She said, "Why don't you go with me?" I called the airline, got a good price, and called Hubby and he said, "Go for it!" I think he was glad NOT to go.

Reservations were changed from one bed to two, however when we arrived all they had was a king-size bed. We decided it shouldn't be a problem. I said, "What do you think of the decorating?" The room had faux timber beams running horizontally and vertically over mirrors extending to the adjacent wall and ceiling. Over the top ugly! I said, "You know, Cathy, it is too bad we aren't lesbians, so we could enjoy this." Cathy laughed her adorable laugh.

I have many "dog" friends. Linda, my Dalmatian partner (we have co-owned and co-bred dogs together for over ten years) is irreplaceable. She has a wicked sense of humor. We play a "mean" game of verbal ping pong!

Cheryl and Judy C. are gals I have co-owned dogs with too, and we love to hang out. We can get a bit wild and crazy when we get together. Cheryl is a sweeter person, but can also "get me." We both love *Dancing with the Stars* and *American Idol.* Her husband, Buddy, is one of my best guy friends. Cheryl has a positive attitude even after going through 14 hours of brain surgery (not cancer) that left her with constant pain running down one side of her body. Six months later she faced uterine cancer surgery and was soon back to work. She always answers her phone with a cherry "Hello."

Mary Lou, my college roommate has gone through a lot: a cheating dentist husband who left her with little money, breast cancer, then treatment for lung cancer. She can hardly talk, but still is cheerful. I admire brave people who remain upbeat. Don't you?

Mary Lou and I have joined former suite mates for several fun reunions. We all almost wet our pants over limericks (humorous five-line rhymed couplets—usually dirty). One of us would write a line or two, pass it on. The more off-color the limericks got, the more fun we had!

My Newfoundland dog friend, Dee, and I met through the Atlanta Kennel Club. We used to go to shows together. I was on my bed, Dee on hers. We were chatting away when all at once, her big boy 150-pound dog really scared me when he decided he was going to jump on my bed. I screamed! Somehow Dee managed to grab him and save me. Thank you, Dee, and thank You, God!

Cute as they are as puppies, Newfy's are a lot of trouble! They can move sofas. Dee is always cleaning up slobber and dog hair. Dalmatian hair stays on the rug, but they love to rub up against you, especially if you are wearing black. Both of us vacuum frequently and don't allow dogs on the furniture. I'm told that my dogs are well behaved. Maybe because I'm "head bitch" at my house.

Dal pals, Judy P. and Joni, are the life of the party type gals. Judy and I really crack each other up. We were walking along, at a dog show, looking like Mutt and Jeff (of the comic strip). Judy is about five foot and I am five-nine. We spotted (good word for Dalmatian pal—ha-ha) Mary Lynn. I love her sense of humor, but we seldom have time to hang out. She was standing ringside with a beautiful, top-quality Chinese Shar-Pei. I said, loud enough for Mary Lynn to hear, "Look Judy, Mary Lynn finally got a good dog." (She actually has had many nice Dals.) She laughed—thank God.

Joni had a sire that produced a lovely litter that I co-bred. She showed two of the puppies to their championship, and her male, Deacon, went on to Best in Show. Joni is a fun mischief-maker. She bought her professional dog handler a special T-shirt that read: LET ME HANDLE YOUR BITCH.

Another special Dal pal is Terri, who went to Kansas City with me in 2009 and 2010. After our annual show in Lawrence, Kansas, in 2010, we stayed in Kansas City to sightsee and share fun with friends Janeyse and Bill. I love hanging out with the "young ones." Dal friends Linda, Helen, Cheryl, and I are all Pisces. Interesting?

Dal pal Julia, pretty and in her mid-forties, while at Dalmatian Club of America shows, asked for fashion advice. She had two dresses with her for our dressy evening event. She liked the cream-colored one with a beaded top, however said, it was "a bit short." "How short is it?" I asked—several times." Finally I said, "Well Julia, if you had a tampon in and no underwear, would you see the string? If not, then it isn't too short." She wore it. She still looked really good. As we left the party, I teased her saying, "It's a good thing you wore it, because next year you'll be too old." Julia is a good sport. I loved seeing her show our boy, now Champion Star Run Atlantis Red Truck.

My friend Claudie, gives me a run for my money. I told her I couldn't love her more unless I was a lesbian. She is short, cute, and "full of it." As she stood on her toes she said, "Let's go for it," and kissed me on the lips. Speechless again!

Someone asked me, "How is it that you have so many girl friends?" I said, "Well I try to be a good friend." I believe in keeping in touch and showing my friends I really care about them. I couldn't tell you who is my best friend. I have a lot of very special gal pals. Thank You, God.

11

Fun Dating in the Stone Age

I grew up in the 50's—the "Stone Age." I was taught nice girls did not have sex before marriage. I had a mother who had scared me to death concerning pregnancy and childbirth. The birth control pill didn't come out until the early 1960s. When I was a teen, we hung out in groups at community events with chaperones. We got to meet a lot of kids. The only dates I had in high school were the junior and senior proms and I had to ask the guys.

There were only 17 in my high school class. I was tall, slender, and (I guess) average looking, but I was taller than most of the boys (5'9"). I also had very high standards. My plans included college and a career. I definitely did not want to become a farmer's wife. This did not keep me from lusting after a guy who was very bright, and a good-looking basketball star.

When I was thirteen, our 4-H Club had a big fundraiser, and all the girls baked cakes to be auctioned off. The highest bidder had the privilege of eating a slice of cake with the girl who had baked it. I made a big chocolate cake with yummy chocolate icing. Can you believe this guy paid $4.10 (about $30 today)? He was a senior when I was in the 8th grade. I later invited him to my senior prom.

When I was about 10, I had a crush on a cute, tall neighbor. I also had mini-crushes on other guys at the 4-H Club Camp. Since I knew I couldn't date until I was 16, nothing ever came of these crushes.

At 17, I started working by selling shoes in the city of Washington Court House, Ohio. My boss's wife owned a shoe store in Wilmington, about 25 miles away. The summer before I went to college I worked at her store. I rented a room in a large Victorian home, and found out being on my own was fun. My landlord expected me in by midnight, and I always was. I was a member of the 4-H Club Band and the community band. Luckily I had several girl friends who lived nearby Wilmington. This was the era before fast food and fast teenagers. At least I didn't know any in our small community. I was brought up to be a good girl and to always do the right thing. Yes, I probably was a goodie two-shoes, but keep in mind I hadn't gone to Ohio State yet.

The summer of 1953 was one of hard work and many responsibilities. I had a key to the store and had to open every morning. Sometimes I was there alone several hours and I worked Monday through Saturday, 9 till 6. I was on my feet all day and I got plenty of exercise reaching up to get the shoes. The shoe store had a large X-ray machine to check children's feet for proper fit. I remember playing on it; I enjoyed seeing my toes wiggle. Today I avoid X-rays. I recall participating in fun community band concerts that summer. I played a mellophone (similar to a French horn) in one band and a cornet in the other. My friends and I often went for refreshments on the walk home. No one my age had a car, so it was a big deal when a teenager was able to borrow the family car.

The 50 mile bus trip to and from Columbus, Ohio, to take modeling classes was starting to pay off. I had more confidence and was less gawky. I remember my older "cake guy" (now 23) took me on a few dates. We had a nice time together. He tried to talk me out of going to college. He said he thought it would "ruin me." Could he have been right? Probably did, in some ways.

That summer I spent a day with a couple of girl friends at a nearby lake, and I got severely sunburned. I recalled the pain that I suffered at work.

Several of my girl friends and I liked to go to the movies. One of them found us "a real deal." The movie theater was having a beauty contest. I knew I wouldn't win, but anyone who participated would be awarded a pass to the movies all summer long. I thought it over long and hard before finally agreeing to participate. I figured probably my grandmother, relatives, and guys I knew wouldn't be there on a week night. I kept thinking about all the movies I could go to. It was really embarrassing, but somehow I received third place out of six. More important, I saw lots of movies with my girl friends.

Soon it was time to pack and leave Ohio for Mary Washington College in Fredericksburg, Virginia. When I was 16, our family had gone to Culpepper, Virginia, to visit Aunt Helen and Uncle Paul. We drove around the University of Virginia college campus. Its beauty won me over. Unfortunately for me, the college did not allow women to attend unless they were nursing students. Women students went to the sister college, Mary Washington. The only men at M.W. were "really old"—late-20s GIs who had served in World War II and were there thanks to the GI Bill and free tuition.

Frankly, the last thing on my mind was dating. I wanted to get through college and be a career woman. I never thought about marriage, even in my future. My ambition was geared towards being the next Ruth Lyons, who was a TV celebrity in Cincinnati, Ohio.

12

Fun with Some of My Girlfriends

In the early 70's, longtime girl friend Elsie and I met over the "lettuce leaves" on Thanksgiving eve. Elsie has a round face and sparkling eyes. I remember she had on a heavy coat and a handmade crocheted hat that made her look like a chipmunk ready to ski. I was wearing layers of clothes since it was "colder than a dead witch's tit," as my college roommate used to say. Elsie overheard me telling T.J. (my 10-year-old son) that I was really cold because I had been in a new, cold, damp, uncompleted house, measuring the windows for blinds and window treatments. Elsie asked if I was in the decorating business. I told her I was, and I worked at Rich's, Atlanta's premier department store.

Elsie asked me to help her with some window treatments. She owned some really nice custom draperies from a previous house that needed re-doing for her new home. Since she sewed, I told her how to do it. She then ordered her custom sheers from me. Not very profitable for Rich's or for me, but I was glad to help her. We quickly became friends.

As I recall, a year later she bought her husband an antique desk for Christmas. Her husband thought this very large package was a huge, new woodworking toy. EVERY TIME he answered the phone or I saw him, I told him I hoped he was buying Elise some wonderful Christmas gifts since she was getting him something extra special. (I always support my girl friends and let their husbands know they are damn lucky guys.)

Elsie and her husband often played bridge with Hubby and me. Their daughter was good friends with our boys. I stopped over late on Christmas Eve afternoon to drop off her Christmas gift. Elsie's husband was home. So once again I was giving the big guy a rough time. I said, "I hope you got Elsie lots of terrific gifts." He replied that he thought he'd better go to Alabama ASAP, which would allow him an extra hour since Alabama is in the Central Time zone. I was teasing him about using Elsie's Halloween broom to fly there.

Elsie had the best Christmas ever. However, "big guy" was NOT thrilled. He was very disappointed he didn't get a new woodworking boy-toy. He never liked the desk. Though he could be a fun guy, I always felt he could have treated Elsie better.

Elsie has always loved antiques and collectables. Since she had a big collection of hats, we decided she should have a bridge party and all the girls would wear her hats. (Women in the 1930s and 40's wore hats and white gloves every time they went out.) Elsie and I both loved and respected my mother-in-law, Rola, who was flying in soon from California. We planned the party when Mom could join us. Recently I came across photos of that party. We look like we were in a weird time warp with our 30's, 40's, and 50's hats, and our 70's funky, funny hippie clothes. That evening the "big guy" was a sweetheart. He willingly filled in since we needed an eighth person. He was a good sport and even wore a sombrero. That evening he was a perfect host and seemed to thoroughly enjoy himself. My husband would have been uncomfortable with all the female chit-chat. The couple later divorced, though. How sad.

Another longtime friend is Karen. She and I met through working together for Davison's department store in Atlanta, in the furniture department. I gave Karen a wedding shower and, a year later, a baby shower. She didn't know her husband long enough before she married him. He started law school and quit working almost as soon as she got pregnant. Karen continued to work, but it was a real strain on her. He was apparently using her. She planned to leave him and go live with her folks on St. Simons Island.

Karen and I hit it off from the beginning. Ada (Karen's best friend) and I had both worked part-time, so the three of us seldom worked together (maybe for a good reason.) We all had a sense of humor and could easily crack each other up. One slow evening we were having a wonderful time. Ada greeted some customers who were shopping for a mattress set. The couple asked us for our opinions. Davison's carried top brands. Price is based on what is inside as well as the cover. All top-of-the-line mattresses are the maker's best (the heaviest coils that are close together). Some have heavy quilted foam tops covered with beautiful luxury fabrics. Heavy, closely woven cotton twill will last longer but does not feel as good when you touch it. Who feels it anyway, when you use a mattress pad to protect the mattress under your sheets? Ada's customers were confused. I remember one of them taking off her shoes and jumping on the mattress to show the firmness. Normally none of us would get involved with someone else's customer or jump on a bed. We did this time and got away with it because the furniture department was in the back of the store and the boss was away. Thank God the customers never complained!

Karen is a terrific artist, with a degree in art from the University of Georgia. She is happily remarried and living on St. Simons. She does beautiful watercolors and pottery.

Years ago, on my way to visit Karen, I was lost again. I had stopped at a grocery store to use a public telephone (before cell phones). I noticed they had a stack of phonebooks with a beautiful watercolor reproduction of a chapel on the front cover. Since the books were free, I took one with me to frame the cover. It was signed *Karen Keene*. Turns out that was Karen's maiden name. I didn't realize it was the same person until I saw the original in her home. We had quite a laugh over it.

I furnished Karen with an arm cap from my French blue country sofa and loveseat. She hand-made lovely blue ceramic lamps, matching the color of my sofa. Years later I still love and use these lamps in my Florida leisure room. Now I have wicker and brightly striped loose cushions. I changed the lampshades and they look perfect. On my memory wall above one of the sofas, hangs a numbered print I bought of the chapel Karen painted. In my dining room is a large, clear glass bowl with lovely ceramic fruit Karen made. I think of her frequently, we talk occasionally, and see each other when possible. Old friends hold a special place in my heart.

One of my newer friends is Maggie whom I met through the Florida Writers Association. Maggie has written several books. One of them, *Amelia's Secrets*, was nominated for a Pulitzer Prize. She is loads of fun and very bright. I have to tell you she is another friend who is an inspiration to me. It is very difficult when you self-publish. She spends two days a week, from ten to five or six in the evening, at book signings usually at Books Plus. She then spends one day a week on research for her new book and two days a week writing. She works at it as a full-time job. She also sells 100 or more books a month. This is very good for an author of a local historical novel.

Maggie is very attractive. When I first met her husband, I started calling him "the hunk" and got them both laughing. Maggie was wearing a nice top and snug black pants. Her husband and I were standing behind her, and I said to him, loud enough for her to hear, "With that cute butt, I can understand why you follow her everywhere."

She not only works hard on writing and selling her books, she is very active in the community. She keeps her house up and even cooks. How's that for a young grandmother?

Aren't girl friends the best?

13

Fun with Guys in Uniform

Don't you just love guys in uniform? I have had some interesting experiences with adorable cops and some not quite so cute. Hey, they don't call me "hot foot" for nothing.

I started driving when I was 21. I have my van checked (tires, brakes, fluid levels) before long trips. I think this is VERY IMPORTANT for everyone, but especially for people who are driving alone or are older.

Before I started using a radar detector, I used to get stopped occasionally. Twice I came close to a ticket, when the "uniforms" got a call they were urgently needed elsewhere. My guardian angels were watching over me.

Youngest son T.J. needed to pick up his car that had come from Europe in Jacksonville, Florida. T.J. had recently returned from a tour of duty in the Air Force. He said, "Mom, I need you to do this, but in order to get down to Jacksonville and back in one day, we need to leave home by 4:00 AM. We didn't return home until after midnight.

T.J. had told me he would drive so I could sleep. I dozed maybe an hour before he woke me and asked me to drive. On the back roads of Georgia I was zipping along when I saw "blue lights." Not a K-Mart special either! I said, "I'm going to try to get out of this."

A large, tough, old southern cop walked up to my window. He said, "Get your license and registration and come get in my car."

I did. I said, "It's my mother, isn't it?"

He said, "What about your mother?"

"She has heart problems (true) and knows I'm on the road (lie). Someone called you about her, right?" (Before cell phones.)

He said, pointing, "No, this is why I stopped you."

I saw the number 78 on his radar monitor on a 55mph road. I said, "Oh thank God, that's all. We're on our way to Jacksonville to see my grandson, who is very ill." (Another lie, I'm afraid.)

I could tell he was not buying it. He started to write out a ticket when he received an emergency call.

He gave me a disgusted look as he handed me my license and registration. He said, "Lady, I really wish I could take you in, but get out of my car, and don't drive over the speed limit."

"Thank you, sir," I said. Man, do I know God answers prayers. But I have to tell you, it shook me up. I didn't drive over the speed limit for about twenty miles! And, I have never told another lie.

On July 3, 2000, I was on my way to Florida in the fast lane. Where else would I be? On this busy, divided six-lane highway, I had slowed down to 70 and was getting ready to move over, to get off at the next exit, when I heard a loud noise, and the van started shaking and was out of control. It was all I could do to hold on! I tried to get off the road but really had no place to go. The median dipped, into a big V (about 10 to 15 feet). I should have pumped the brake, but didn't as I just wanted it to STOP! It was July 3rd and all three lanes were very crowded and everyone was speeding.

Instantly I went into the ditch and was alarmed I was heading towards oncoming traffic. I turned the wheel, and the van turned over—on the driver's side. The van was crushed in about two feet on my side, windshield broken and I was hurt. The EMTs pushed a smaller guy through the front window so he could push on my butt (embarrassing) to get me out. Those EMTs were wonderful. After they put me on a stretcher, they had to deal with my dog. Her crate was well tied down. When the van turned over, the stainless steel door popped off the plastic crate.

One of the EMTs took her to his vet. My-My was in show condition with her nails short and facial hair cut off. The vet had to know she was loved. The next morning he drove 30 miles to deliver her to the motel where I stayed overnight. He said she was sore and had a few bruises, but otherwise she was fine. Bless his heart! He never let me pay him anything. Perhaps he saw my bloody face and what condition I was in and decided against it. I later sent him some Omaha Steaks. Thank God for people like him!

My near-death experience left me with several broken ribs on either side of the seat belt, and two vertebras in my back. Without a seat belt, I wouldn't be here. Hubby did not realize what bad shape I was in. I didn't realize it myself until the middle of the night, when the pain set in. My van was very full because we were moving. The heat of the pavement, the extra weight, and my speed probably all contributed to the accident.

The next week was the most horrible of my life. Cancer or kidney failure was nothing compared to a couple of days <u>after</u> broken bones. But thanks to the "uniforms," a very good second doctor, and Hubby, I made it. For some reason, the third day after an accident or surgery seems the worst. Because I had kidney failure 10 years before, I have to drink at least eight glasses of water a day. So EVERY time I had to get up, I had to call Hubby to help me. Not easy for us, as I was in A LOT of pain and crying! It got old <u>real fast</u>! One thing you might find amusing is, while the EMTs were waiting for the ambulance, I was telling them the latest Monica jokes. I was making the best of a bad situation.

Recently my TOPS buddies and I were coming out of our meeting (which met in the same building as the Police Department) when we noticed a young, cute male officer walking by. I said to our leader, Marie, "Look how cute our officers are getting." We could see his neck turn red. The gals chuckled. I just try to make people happy. Guys love to hear they are cute. I love to see them blush, and my friends laugh, so we hit a trifecta.

The last speeding ticket I received was at 2:30 AM. I felt like asking the young, cute "uniform" if his mama knew where he was. However, I was so anxious to get this over with that I accepted my ticket and went on my way.

The $250.00 fine and points on my license MADE me get a radar detector. They keep changing the technology, so I need to update every few years. I know this because Hubby is always working for the other side—inventing better radar. No, he does not approve of my using a radar detector. I know I do <u>a lot</u> of things he doesn't approve of! What else is new?

My friend, Faye, and I were in a local restaurant several years ago, when I noticed some handsome "uniforms" (EMTs). I said to Faye, loud enough for them to hear, "Faye, I wonder what we have to do to get rescued?" They grinned.

I'm always thanking our men and women in uniform for serving our community or our country. It must be so hard on them to be away from their families sometimes for months or years involved in tricky local or global situations.

Years ago I was driving from Roswell, Georgia, to a house we used to have in Palm Harbor, Florida. I was really speeding along as I had a Dalmatian in labor, and I got pulled over. The officer wanted me to follow him to a vet's office. I said, "No, I have delivered a lot of puppies. I just need to get her home." I can't recall if I got a ticket or not, but I barely made it.

The first puppy arrived about 20 minutes after I arrived home. Top Spot, their father, was so cute with them. He let me know when I needed to help get the next one out. He never left mama Bubbles side. He was wonderful with the puppies. Maybe I should have dressed him in a little doggie doctor outfit.

Not long ago our Florida Writers Association group asked author Bruce Thomason, who wrote Death Toll, to come talk to us. What a nice-looking guy. Just think, he sometimes wears a uniform. He is Chief of Police at another beach town. If you saw him as we did, in a sports jacket, you might think he was a college professor.

He was putting his books on a table.

I said, "Are you our author for tonight?"

"Yes," he said in a soft, cultured voice.

I said, "Maggie didn't tell us you were so cute."

Guess what? He blushed.

He told us about writing Death Toll and a new book he was working on.

Then he said, "I was surprised to find out from my book signing, the majority of the e-mail addresses given were women's. I would have thought my book would attract mostly men."

I could not help myself. I said, "It's because you're so cute that women want to buy your books."

He blushed again.

Later on he asked for questions and answered several. I put my hand up, he looked at me, hesitated, and blushed.

I said, "You're afraid of me, aren't you?"

He said, "Sort of," as he blushed.

Guess what? Several months later I ran into him with his fun, attractive wife at a writer's conference.

And then there is another "uniform" story about a cute sailor I dated during my freshman year in college. . . . . But that's another story.

14

Fun with The Queen

Yes, I saw her! The Queen of England. I was about ten feet away as she and Prince Philip came out of the Palace gates in a large black limo. O.K. I didn't meet her, but I was closer than some English people ever get. She was surprisingly beautiful, in her mid-forties with porcelain like skin. I was surprised at not only how lovely she was, but also how small. Being short-waisted with large boobs made her look somewhat dumpy in photos. I feel she probably wore a size six, at most. I was so taken with her I didn't pay much attention to Prince Philip, even though I had a sort of crush on him.

I had met Sarah, a Yorkie breeder, through the Atlanta Kennel Club. Sarah told me about the doggie chartered plane tours. We flew from Atlanta to New York and on to London. There were maybe around a hundred on the plane. I had fun as I went up and down the aisles meeting everyone and looking for Dalmatian people.

The dog show took up three days of our time. However we had several extra days for sightseeing and shopping. When I am in a new city I love to go to department stores and look around. You can learn a lot about the people by the merchandise. For instance on another trip, in Paris, I noticed a large area taken up by Dr. Scholl's products. Style and high heels bring on all sorts of feet problems, don't they?

At the train station, I asked Sarah if she minded if I didn't go to the country with her to see a Yorkie Breeder. She didn't. Since the palace was nearby I went to see "the changing of the guard." Walking along I asked an older guy carrying a large CBS camera how to get to the palace. He said I could walk over with him as he was going there. He was from the U.S. living and working in England. When we got there he said, "Something is going on. The Queen's special honor guard is out. "Maybe the Queen is going to appear."

I stood near the big gates and soon out came the limo. I am really close (4-6 ft.) The queen wore a robin-egg blue wool coat with a matching hat that was awesome with her blue eyes and lovely skin. The TV guy told me a few minutes later he had missed getting close enough. Afterwards, as I walked away, I saw three feet away, Lauren Bacall, (a very famous actress in the 1940's) getting into a cab. She was doing a play in London. She had on a grey fitted mid-calf coat with high heeled black boots. She was very thin and not as beautiful as the queen. Think of it—seeing the two within about fifteen minutes. I spent the rest of the day at the wonderful Tate Museum. A must see for all the Impressionist paintings.

On the bus I sat next to a lady who told me that it was her 80th birthday. I got up and told everyone, and lead them in singing "Happy Birthday." She blushed, bless her heart. Those English people are so much fun!

Late afternoon, I always went to the hotel pub to meet up with people from our "puppy plane." (Some of the people would bring dogs and puppies back since it was a charter flight.) I would decide which play I wanted to see and persuaded others to go with me. We would share a cab and buy inexpensive tickets. Surprise, surprise I choose British comedies. Every day we got a big English breakfast with our room and I would skip lunch. Late afternoon I would pick up a sandwich. This saved time and money. The plays were wonderful! I do so love the English sense of humor!

One of the plays was set in a grand estate. The elderly couple were having breakfast and reading the paper. The lady of the manor was a conservationist. It seems the government was planning on cutting down a lot of trees on their estate for an expressway. She tells her husband she is prepared to die if necessary to save the trees. Like so many men he doesn't even hear her. As I recall she sends letters of protest and gets a letter to the editor published. She does all she can do, but it appears nothing can be done. She told her son she would chain herself to a tree. He didn't take her seriously. She decided she would end up dying chained to a tree. She calls in the coffin maker. (Of course the Lady of the Manor will have a custom coffin!) The next day, she is holding various samples of fabric up to her face and asking family members which color looks best. As funny as I found it, the English laughed more.

At Crufts (the world's largest dog show) they had benches around the square ring—no ropes. The dogs weren't as well groomed as ours and the Dalmatians were larger. I had gotten the name and phone number of the President of the British Dalmatian Club and gave her a call. She told me that most exhibitors only kept a couple of house dogs. I had hoped to visit some breeders, but it didn't happen. The next day the Dal people served us a mug of hot hearty soup and a sandwich. Wasn't that sweet?

The first day I saw mostly working breeds and I visited with some of the vendors. One was a lady artist who did pencil drawings of dogs. At another booth I met Barbara Woodhouse, a neat lady who wrote books on dog training. She told me that her books were to be published and promoted in the states. I invited her to come to Atlanta and stay with us. A little over a year later she and her husband (a retired doctor) were with us, for a week. The lady artist came as well. Word of advice, don't ask an English person to come see you unless you are really serious. All was fine with Barbara and her husband. However, they completely wore me out. I was so exhausted from running them around, that I overslept and missed a luncheon the next day. I was happy to do it, but the BIG TIME publisher never offered to help with gas or food expenses. Barbara treated me to lunch out and gave me a signed book.

The artist was another story. I had splurged on a nice roast, only to find out she was a vegetarian. She was very sweet, but I wasn't prepared. We appreciated a lovely drawing she did of our first homebred champion.

Traveling home from England I stopped in New York to attend the Westminster show. I was to room with a Dal friend from California. Arriving around midnight, I was told she wasn't registered. (She was, it turned out.) What was I to do? There were no rooms available. A lady from Athens, GA, also there for shows, offered to let me room with her. Thank God!

She and I flew home on the same small plane that was to land in Charlotte, Athens and Atlanta. However, when we got to Atlanta the pilot couldn't get the landing gear to go down. We circled the airport. Finally he announced that we would have an emergency landing. (NOT words you want to hear.) The runway was foamed and out came emergency fire trucks, etc . . . were ready. At the last moment the landing gear finally went down. Thank you God! My ten and thirteen year old boys got their mom back. My husband and dogs seemed happy I made it. I know I was. Thank you God!

15

Fun Trying to Stay Young

My Dalmatian pal Lucy, whom I have known for over forty years, asked me if I was a "cougar." I say, "No, Lucy I am a "want a be, but never will be a cougar." Let's face it—younger faces and bodies are more attractive. This is why some middle age guys and gals like to be with much younger partners. All of this I think is due to, one day you are thirty and the next fifty. Or at least it seems that way. You don't want the fun things to stop. You feel however as if they are stopping. Maybe that feeling is a mid-life crisis. Some people, usually guys, find they have to have a sports car or a motorcycle. Or they make a fool of themselves and are embarrassing. Often they don't seem to know it. This is often apparent after a few drinks.

God does seem to have a sense of humor. Just as we are getting our act together and understanding what life is about, weird things happen to us. Men find hair on their heads slipping to ears and noses. Women don't have it easier as gravity takes effect. You know you have reached this stage when you prefer elastic waist pants. You know it happened to you while you were sleeping. Or, maybe you have put your panties on before your bra, and you "happen" to zip up your boobs.

"Old age isn't for sissies," as my dad said. Before you know it, you are older. Most people never feel mentally over thirty-five. At times it is very surprising to look in the mirror and see this old person.

Being over seventy, I can tell you one good thing about old age is that it evens out life. A-lot of those cute little cheerleader types that never went through the awkward stages, are now short and fat, and aren't so cute anymore. One of my older friends told me that she used to have dimples. However they have now turned into wrinkles. I said, (the bad girl that I am) "There is a God" as we grinned at each other. I told her that when I was little, I wanted dimples so badly that I walked around with my fingers poked in my face. I must have been six or seven at the time so I have no idea how long this went on. I wanted them until I started getting pimples.

One of my special friends is Viv, a very attractive over eighty gal. She looks and acts much younger. She stands straight and could pass from, the rear, as someone at least twenty years younger. She plays tennis twice a week and hikes five miles. She does her make-up, keeps her hair and brows red, and her nails painted. She reads good books. Along with her husband they keep their house clean. She cooks and keeps up her flower garden. She is truly a big inspiration for me! Did I mention that forty year olds would look fashionable in her clothes? Or that she wears the same size clothes as she did in college. If she weren't so much fun she could be easy to hate. I'm ten years younger and no, I can't keep up with her, but I keep trying and trying.

I've often thought about what makes Viv different than most women her age. I believe it is her young attitude, staying active, and staying attractive. She attends church regularly and yet she can still tell a good dirty joke. Viv does have a few wrinkles, but people have guessed her age as below sixty. Isn't that cool?

Have to tell you about Viv's husband. They met in the first grade, and in third grade he put a snake down her back. If you think they were always in love, wrong. Les was a really handsome young man and married his childhood sweetheart for 20 years. A quick rebound marriage lasted three years. The third marriage was good however, but she died of cancer. Viv didn't marry until she was twenty seven. Two years later they were divorced. She met the love of her life, and had two children. After about twenty years, he died.

Viv and Les often went back to Minnesota for class reunions. This time they were both single. They hung out together and had a great time! Les had a home in North Carolina, Viv in New Orleans. Les was depressed after losing his wife. Viv spiced up his life. Soon they were married. This was about nine years ago. He told us last summer, a month before he died of a massive heart attack, that he was the happiest he has ever been. How they kept up the garden and house was amazing, as they were always on the go. I find it very funny that while they were in North Carolina they went to the Baptist church, yet in New Orleans they went to the Presbyterian Church.

I tell my younger single friends love and marriage are all about timing. As one of my friends tells me, sometimes an older man is worth the trouble. A man who is really lonesome, a good person and appreciates a good woman, can sometimes be the one who "adores" a younger woman. Myself, I've been married over fifty years and I'd like a fifty year old. (Ha Ha) This is when Lucy asked, "Emily Hoover, are you a cougar?"

I also have a couple of over ninety year old bridge buddies. They are both sharp gals with great attitudes who keep themselves attractive mentally and physically. Charlotte keeps her red hair, and always looks fashionable. Wilda has gorgeous white hair and is more of the casual type. These gals are often top winners at bridge. If you take care of yourself, keep your weight under control, not only will you feel better, but you will live longer. This includes exercise, eating right and keeping God in your life. You can be fun, fit, and fabulous. If you don't keep healthy you can look forward to health concerns. That means cancer, diabetes, and/or heart problems. You can easily end up in a nursing home. I try to remember what Dr. Phil says, "You can get real about fat or get real fat." I attend TOPS (Take off Pounds Sensibly) every week. I say, "Go to Curves, or lose your curves." As to keeping weight off it is all about reasonable servings, enjoying each bite, chewing slowly and getting enough exercise.

Stay young by taking care of yourself, mentally and physically.

P.S.—Our North Carolina Friendship Club is having a luncheon/meeting/surprise birthday party August 5, 2011, for our good friend Charlotte who will be 98! I will be reading this chapter. We are planning a cake, cards and flowers.

I hadn't seen Charlotte since last October. What a gal! She probably has a special bond with all of her friends. We both love fun and to tease. I feel we have a special relationship.

She walks into the restaurant, looking great in a sunny yellow jacket matching her radiant smile. She asks me if my book is done YET? Once again, she "got" me by bragging about winning again at bridge. Damn! I've only won first TWICE in my life. What a woman! The first five minutes and she "got" me twice. How I love and appreciate her. She is charming, outgoing, interesting, well read and fun to be around. She is a great grandmother to twin teen boys and I bet they love hanging out with her. What probably makes her so special is that she is SO interested and caring of others.

She told us her secret to long life was playing bridge, playing with her little dog and keeping house and cooking. She still lives alone with her little dog. I hear that she recently told a mutual friend that she and her dog are having a contest to see who can outlive the other, and that they are neck and neck. Is that funny? Love her! Hope I get invited to her 100th!

16

Fun with God and the Internet

In Genesis 21:1-6 we find an example of God's humor. It seems that Sarah had always wanted to be a mother. God promised her a son, but the son wasn't conceived until Sarah was in old age. The father, Isaac, was reportedly one hundred years old. Sarah says, "God has brought laughter for me; everyone who hears will laugh with me."

I say as a mother I don't understand! What the hell was God thinking anyway? I had enough problems being a young and energetic mother at 24 and 27. So God, couldn't you have gotten creative with another miracle? I am now seventy-five and frankly God if you did this to me, I would probably commit the biggest sin of all—suicide.

However I am trying to look at this in an objective way. Logically I feel that whoever wrote that passage in the bible must have been bad at math. I sure don't see giving old people babies. I feel parents need to be young and healthy to raise kids.

If I were to do it over again, I would be thirty before I married and thirty-three before I had kids. I feel kids need stable parents, with good ethics and in a good financial position and, hopefully, can raise the children themselves. Hey guys, those little suckers are expensive! They also require a lot of attention! They are me, me, ME little people. Very demanding! Guess what; even when they are fifty you still worry about them. Once a mother, always a mother. Fathers get concerned at times, but aren't as connected.

Years ago while on vacation, I attended a church that had an attractive young minister. The assistant minister was her husband. Someone later told me that one Sunday they stood in front of their congregation and told them they were separating. She stayed at the church. He moved to another church a few hundred miles away. When he remarried, guess who married them? She did. Isn't that the ultimate in forgiveness?

On the lighter side, have you seen the cartoon of a man driving and texting, with a woman saying, "Honk if you love Jesus . . . Text while driving if you want to meet him." Mr. Reynold did it. It came off the internet. I thought it was wonderful, and so true. Please don't text and drive. Don't drink and drive either.

Internet jokes—source unfortunately was not given, maybe for a good reason.

Weight watchers will meet at 7pm. Please use the large double doors at the side entrance.

Ladies, don't forget the rummage sale. It is a good chance to get rid of those things not worth keeping around the house. Bring your husbands.

The sermon this morning: "Jesus walks on the water." The sermon tonight: "Searching for Jesus."

Interesting? If you have ever been in a choir—especially a church choir—you should enjoy these T.J.

The pastor will preach his farewell message, after which the choir will sing, "Break Forth into Joy."

Today's sermon: "How much can a person drink? With hymns from a full choir."

Next Thursday there will be tryouts for the choir. They need all the help they can get.

Our next song is "Angels We Have Heard Get High."

The choir will disrobe for the summer months and join us in the pews.

The "Over 60's Choir" will be disbanded for the summer with the thanks of the entire church.

I have never been in a church choir, but all the people I met that are, seem to be really fun. I do know that choirs everywhere seem to have good parties with lots of great food. I'm ready to join up

I think the following is very funny. How about you?

Barbara remains in the hospital and needs blood donors for more transfusions. She is also having trouble sleeping and request tapes of Pastor Jack's sermons.

Hey pastors are any of these internet goodies coming from your bulletins? What kind of typist do you have anyway? Can't he or she use spell check?

Next Sunday the service will feature a guitarist who can sin and play at the same time.

Attend and you will hear an excellent speaker and heave a healthy lunch.

Oh goodie we get to vomit.

The senior choir invited any member of the congregation who enjoys sinning to join the choir.

I love, love, love this one!

This evening at 7pm there will be a hymn sing in the park across from the Church. Bring a blanket and come prepared to sin.

Isn't this group sex? Somehow I don't think God would promote it—Do you?

17

Fun with Dalmatian Gal Pals

I have known Helen, a pretty, single, brunette for about 20 years. We have a lot of fun together. Helen went through a period when she really wanted to meet "The One" before her biological clock ran out. Frequently she drove from Knoxville down to Roswell, Georgia, and stayed with Hubby and me for the weekend.

Helen always cleaned up after herself and stripped the bed. We got a kick out of her, especially when she watched a U.T. football game. You'd think the players could hear her instructions.

After Helen acquired a cell phone she'd call me especially at Christmastime. I asked if she still had a set of bedding with a moose motif she had been given the year before. She said she had them on her guest bed.

Then we talked about her Christmas plans. I said, "I'm sorry I haven't sent your gift as I had to get it out of layaway." She asked what it was, but I wouldn't say and kept changing the subject. She continued asking me, and I said she'd find out when she got home and changed the subject. Then she asked, "Not a dog is it?" I said, "I never would do that to *anyone*." I changed the subject. I finally said, "It came from an antique shop." She begged me to tell her. I finally told her it was a moose head. She said, "Is it alive?" "Not anymore." She said, "You shouldn't have." I couldn't tell if she was being the Southern Lady or what.

"Nothing is too good for our Helen. I knew you liked moose, so when I saw it at a reduced price, I just had to get it." She said, "You really shouldn't have." Again: "Nothing is too good for our Helen." I asked her where she'd put it. She said, "I'm not sure. They really look best in really large rooms . . . like a lodge." Then I said, "Why don't you hang it over your guest bed? It goes with the other moose stuff." She said, "Oh, I couldn't. My sister is coming for her veterinarian reunion. I don't want to offend her. You really didn't get me a moose head, did you?" I told her, "No, but I 'got' you, didn't I?"

When her 40th birthday was coming up and I wanted to have some fun. I called our mutual friend, Linda (my vet Dal pal that I co-owned Dalmatians with) and asked her advice. I said, "Maybe we should send her thong underwear since she mentioned that she's now wearing them." After some discussion we figured out her size. Linda said she would get a red pair and a card and mail them from another town.

As it happened, my grade-school friend, Joy Wilson (whom I had not seen, written, or talked to in 56 years), had called me and came for a visit. We went shopping and I told her of our plan. We had fun shopping deals on cards and underwear. I had Joy write Helen's address on a couple of envelopes—changing pens—writing on one, printing on another, etc. I had my son T.J. and grandson J.D. do a few as well. They signed them "From an Old Beau," "From someone who wants to get to know you better," "XOXO from Guess Who?" Man, were we creative. I placed some of them in larger envelopes and mailed them to our nieces in California. A friend went to Puerto Rico and mailed one. Joy took two with her and sent one from Dayton and another from Cincinnati.

The first thongs to arrive were the ones from Linda. (Victoria's Secret, red and very nice.) Guess what? Helen called and asked if I had sent them. Can you imagine; Joy was here at the time so it was difficult to talk to Helen without laughing. I told her, "No, I didn't send those." As it happens, Helen is no dummy. She had looked at the postmark and learned it was near where one of our sons lives. She asked me if I had him send them for me. "No, I didn't. Would I lie to you?" That put her on the spot. (Good phrase—get it?—Dalmatians.) She had to say no, she didn't think so, "but you like to do pranks." I acted offended. Joy was grinning.

A week later Helen received another pair, and a few days later, more. I told her, "This is driving me crazy. Who would do this to you? I want to know." I convinced her it wasn't me. Well, I had not sent her any myself, yet. She came home from a business trip and two more pairs had arrived. Also, she recognized an old beau's phone number on her caller ID and figured it was him. I asked, "Are you going to call and ask him?" "HEAVENS NO!" In about eight weeks she had received "12 pair." She was calling me every other day. So far she couldn't figure it out from the postmarks. The last one I sent included a picture of a guy in a Dalmatian suit. I had printed: THIS MAY BE ME OR MAYBE NOT.

She called and said, "I knew it was you!" I said, "Just how did I get all over the place to mail them?" She said, "I don't know how you did it, but I would almost bet my life on it. I know it's your writing." I said, "No, it isn't my writing." (However, it was my printing.) Finally I told her, "Yes, but I "got you" didn't I?"

Then she went on to say that it was expensive to do. I said, "Nothing is too good for our Helen." I told her I got all the panties on sale and a couple were sent from other friends. To throw her off, I had already sent her a birthday gift. All the rest I had sent to other people with the stamped envelopes for them to mail. So yes, it did cost me a few dollars, but remember, nothing is too good for our Helen.

It was the best joke I have ever played on anyone and went on for eight weeks. What fun! As you can see, I don't just have fun with "the guys."

Who said, "God gave us friends for putting up with our relatives"? Really?

Another fun, fun, fun Dal pal is my friend Lucy. I met her at a dog show over 40 years ago. Lucy and Dal pal Cheryl both have the most wonderful laughs. Lucy's is a wicked "I'll 'get you'" giggle, where Cheryl has a "My gosh, you 'got me'" belly laugh. I really should record them so I can listen to them when I'm dying. I'm not planning that soon, but who plans, anyway? Both can make me belly laugh—and that is not easy.

The most trouble I ever got into was because of Lucy. We had recently formed The Dalmatian Club of Greater Atlanta and had a member who, apparently, Lucy and this other gal thought needed to "lighten up." I remember that Lucy started talking about how you can see photos of dogs that make them look different than they actually look. Lucy said maybe we should have a Dalmatian Dog Museum where the top winning dogs were stuffed (gross, yes). I had been asked "to go along" with Lucy. This lady was appalled. Lucy said, "Emily, don't you think it would be great to have 'Black Diamond' on display for generations to come?" At this point I was thinking, how can I make this funny? Our friend had a very nice champion, "Rex." So I said, "Maybe it would be a good idea to have 'Rex' stuffed too." They agreed. I said that maybe we could stuff the owners and display them next to their dogs. That "got" them. What could they do but laugh?

A few months later we had gone to Ohio and brought home "King." King was a Saint Bernard who had belonged to an uncle of my cousin's wife. When King died, he was made into a rug (like a bear rug). My cousin Lowell had a lot of fun with him. His brother, Claire, taught night adult classes. Claire had left his car unlocked, as we all did years ago. Lowell put King's head and front paws on the steering wheel. It shook up Claire, I hear. We put him on the top bunk in S.C.'s room to keep him away from the Dals, and to await his entrance into Atlanta society.

I heard Lucy and her husband were coming in from Alabama for our next Dal meeting. I told our friend we would all be there. After the meeting and dinner I had one of our sons bring me King. I came into the room on my hands and knees with King draped over me. Well, my friends thought it was very funny. However, not everyone. Someone called the next day and said the pregnant gal wasn't feeling well afterwards. Bless her heart, I phoned those I offended and apologized. Not that I would ever have a dog made into a rug. I thought it was gross, but what I did with the rug remains very funny in Lucy's mind.

In the late 60's we held our National Specialty show in Lexington and had our show on the grounds of a lovely hotel there. I checked out but wouldn't be leaving until late. Lucy is something! She has a lot more nerve than I do. We were sitting around the pool having a good time. Lucy said, loud enough for most people to hear, "I'm doing a study of belly buttons. I want to see if you guys have an 'innie' or an 'outie.'" She proceeded to go around looking at guys' belly buttons. One guy blushed from his waist to the top of his bald head.

After awhile a couple of us went back to the room we were sharing. There was Lucy crawling around in the bathroom on her knees. When we asked Lucy what she was doing, she said, "I can't find my contact lenses. I thought I put them in the glass by the sink. Maybe they fell on the floor. No, I know I put them in a glass. Where did the glass go?" Someone said, "I bet Steve put ice and a drink in it and gave it to someone." "Oh no!" said Lucy. I said, "Well, look on the bright side, maybe someone now has a seeing-eye belly button." Lucy laughed, however, she never found them.

In the 70's or 80's a PhD did a paper on people and their dogs, titled "Why do we choose certain breeds?" He said most often there are psychological reasons behind our choices. He said Dachshund and Dalmatian people are usually "the life of the party." YES, YES, YES! When there are several of us together, we can and do egg each other on. What fun! Can you see why I like to go to dog shows? I have friends in other breeds, but my Dal pals are predictably more fun! It is a nonjudgmental, freeing experience to be with them.

Hubby is very good with my gal pals—though I think he can take only one at a time.

Dal pals Linda, Cheryl, Judy C., Judy P, Joni, Terri, and I try to get together at some of our Southern shows. Joni has a quick wit and is ready for fun. She gets the rest of us going. Any combo of the above and one drink does it—for a really great time! We haven't been asked to leave any restaurant yet, but it very well could happen. We, like our dogs, are probably "too much" for a lot of people. To be with one gal Dal pal is a lot of fun and to be with several at a time is an absolute ball. The stories we can come up with. You have no idea: bad, bad, bad!

18

Fun Traveling

Yes, I have fun flying in spite of all the irritations.

Some of you remember when we dressed up for a flight. Women wore girdles (ugh, ugh, ugh), hose, dresses, and heels. Rubber girdles were HOT and horrible! I remember one cutting in on my thighs. Most women wore hats and gloves. Men looked handsome in business suits, shirts, and ties. Flying was a big deal and expensive.

To attend modeling school I took a bus for a 50-mile trip from London, Ohio, to Columbus and later, after I transferred colleges, to Ohio State. In 1953 when I was a freshman at Mary Washington College in Fredericksburg, Virginia, I took a train home for Christmas vacation. I sat next to a really cute sailor whom I was soon dating. This is before planes were an option.

In the early 50's Hubby took a bus back and forth from Columbus, Ohio, to visit his mom in St. Petersburg, Florida. The trip took 24 hours, stopping at every little town.

After college graduation my future husband ended up moving to Florida. In fact, my first airline flight was to go visit him at Easter time (1958). Most of you are thinking "fun in the sun and in the sack." I stayed in a motel, not his apartment. This "good girl" didn't "do it" until marriage; I had high morals and this was before birth control pills. Back to my flight. Get this: I had to change planes—and airlines—three times. I left early in the morning, and it was getting dark as we landed in Tampa.

Now, due to my husband's semi-retirement and the deals our youngest son has found, we can afford to travel more.

Sometimes it pays to be nice or fun. Joking around can work too. On a trip to Rome several years ago we arrived at the Atlanta airport early a.m., and there was a boarding delay. Fortunately I had taken a couple of sandwiches. Finally we boarded the plane, only to face more delays. Later we were asked to de-plane, but remain in the boarding area.

While we waited, I thought about my wardrobe. Did I bring everything I needed? My friend Elsie told me to pack three days before a trip. This gives me time to remove anything unnecessary. I use my portable clothes rack to sort out my outfits and plan carefully. Laundry facilities aren't always available. I wear black and take some bright tops.

If going to Europe, I take voltage converters for hair dryers and my small air filter (always examined by security). The air filter not only helps alleviate allergy problems but also filters out hotel and people noises (such as Hubby's snoring). Hey, are you seeing that it can't be easy traveling, rooming, or being married to me? I love to go places, but I am <u>not a very good traveler</u>.

Back to the waiting game. Late afternoon the airline announced we needed to rebook our flights. Fortunately, the airline employee who had checked us in, remembered us. I said, "This is a pain in the butt for you, isn't it?" She grinned and said, "That's my job." She also said there were no more flights that evening.

Not good news. This meant we'd miss our grandson's graduation. (His dad had paid for J.D. to attend his last year in high school in Lanciano, Italy, at an international school. We had argued against it, but T.J. thought it would be a great cultural experience. That turned out to be true, and J.D. loved it.)

While I was joking with the airline representative, I said to Hubby, "Maybe this lovely lady will upgrade us to first class." She laughed and said, "I can't get you into first class, but maybe I can get you into business class, which has recliner seats." She also arranged for the airline to compensate us for a room overnight. Going business-class was great. It was super to get a steak done medium rare. Do you think everyone received such an upgrade?

Occasionally, with God's help, I get really lucky.

19

Fun Being Illegally Blonde

Until now, only my hairdresser knew for sure that I may not be illegally blonde, but I am blonde by choice. I have several blonde by choice friends. According to one of my friends, a lot of unforgettable things happen to me. Could it be because I'm blonde???

When Hubby was very young, he started delivering newspapers. In high school he worked as a soda jerk. (Google that one, young ones.) Later he bagged groceries as he saved money for college. Hubby has since developed all kinds of antennas, microwaves, and ferrite systems. And guess what? He still, at 78, works part-time at home or in Atlanta. In the late '60s, after our move from California to Atlanta, Hubby worked every day from 8-5. Then after dinner Monday-Thursday he went back to work another 3 hours. On Saturdays he worked four more hours. Some weekends he took off to go Boy Scott camping with our sons. He deserved a special car.

One day Hubby was driving my van, and I had his car. Not just any car, but the first really posh car he ever had. To say he loved it more than me is an understatement. It was a conservative gray and it was a French Peugeot. Oh, those wonderful gray leather seats that could be heated. They were wide, tall and adjustable with plenty of leg room. I don't know of ANY vehicle that was as comfortable. The dashboard lit up like a Christmas tree. Riding in the Peugeot was like riding on whipped cream. When you arrived anywhere—even the local dump—you arrived in style. After all, it was French! Think of it—travelling across the ocean so Hubby could buy and love it. He loved, loved, loved that car, and deserved it too!

What he didn't deserve, was what I did to his beloved vehicle. How he came to trust me with it, even for one day, is amazing. The accident I had was a real NIGHTMARE. All I remember is driving into our carport and suddenly my right foot slipped from the "brake" to the "gas" pedal. All I wanted to do was STOP, STOP, STOP! The next thing that happened was like the beginning of a bad movie. The front end of the car hit a tall, black metal shelving unit. In slow motion I saw it bend slowly, slowly, slowly falling over the front end of Hubby's precious car. Oh me, oh my, NOT GOOD! OH SHIT! DAMN! HELL! Not fun. The car finally stopped, I got out. All was NOT good! One headlight GONE, front bumper GONE, and the top of the hood was covered with goo—Big-time GOO. Oil, maybe?

I went into the house in a state of shock. Shaking, I phoned Hubby. Is this what dumb or illegally blondes feel like?

Fortunately, I reached his voicemail. I left the following message: "Honey, I had an accident but NO ONE was hurt. I'm home."

Soon—too soon—Hubby called. He was NOT happy. He told me he was on his way home—and that he had to be back soon for a meeting.

He got home and looked over the situation. Then he said, "Did you see what you did to the brick wall?" I had to say "No." I looked and stood there stunned at what I saw, as he went into the house. Some of the bricks were messed up and some lay "broken-hearted" on the floor, like my heart. Inside the living / dining room, my pretty peach wall had a huge crack running from the ceiling to the floor. I could see broken two-by-fours. Shit, damn, hell! Not a good day at the Hoover house. Boy, was Hubby upset! However, he didn't say much as he cleaned off the goop. But man did he frown! Now Hubby has lots of frown wrinkles. Maybe you wonder why. Oh, that's right. You know, don't you? It was an expensive accident, but no one was hurt.

When my Red Hat Society blonde friend, Lori, told me she had a very similar accident, I couldn't believe it. Her foot slipped, just like mine. When she hit her wall, it caused her china cabinet, full of expensive Waterford crystal, to break! Her husband, who had recently died, had bought the crystal in Ireland. It had been shipped over here to become "just a memory." Worse, it wasn't insured. Lori was as broken as her crystal. What a mess!

We both have worked as interior decorators, we are both fun, we both were dog people and we both had "the same" stupid accident. And guess what? We are both "blonde by choice."

The interesting thing was that Hubby, who doesn't normally get excited, got REAL excited. Thank God he is NOT the violent type. I don't think <u>anyone</u> should tolerate abuse. If anyone mistreats you—REGARDLESS of ANYTHING <u>they say</u>—they DON'T love you. ACTIONS always speak louder than words!

I have to tell you, blondes has been more fun. People don't expect as much from blondes. If you are smart, or a smart-ass like me, you will surprise people. Surprise is always good.

20

Fun with Chelsea Handler

I love, love, love the Sunday edition of the New York Times. On the front of the Style Section is Chelsea with her amazing blue eyes-staring straight at me. What a cutie! She is a late night hottie, on the E channel. On her show, "Chelsea Lately," she does about 5 minutes of topical humor, then is joined by various members of her comedian/writers staff. They each comment, trying to outdo each other, and generally trash any celebrity who has been behaving badly. Then Chelsea, in her amusing style, interviews interesting people who are promoting a new book, TV show, or movie. Her show could be called "Private Parts."

Last summer Chelsea had THREE books on the New York Times Best Seller List and now another. She tours every weekend doing stand-up. She is a hot topic of conversations like Ernest Hemingway supposedly was in his day. Who said, "The most essential gift for a good writer is a built in-shock proof shit detector"?

Maybe you need to know I was not an English major—or minor, either, maybe an English "mindless." I hired an excellent typist and professional editor, but I'm pretty sure neither of them owns a shit detector. I don't even know what one looks like, do you? I do know I am *not* in Hemingway's league.

Too bad Hemingway is dead, because I could see him, Chelsea Handler, and myself hanging out at a bar and grill in Key West. I'd be enjoying a steak, salad, baked potato, key lime pie, and a couple of drinks while those two would be drinking, drinking, drinking away. I'd be listening to every word they would be saying and probably laugh a lot. (Too bad I can't fake being an intellectual.) As the sun turns tangerine and the waters a dark aqua, Chelsea and Ernest are enjoying playing verbal ping-pong. I soon leave as I see Chelsea "wanting to score" kind of like a Best in Show bitch in "standing heat." Can't you just hear her saying "Bring it on Big Daddy?"

Chelsea is like a beautiful Best in Show Bitch while Ernest would be a pet quality bloodhound with a BIG belly and a BIG attitude.

Chelsea and I have a lot in common. We both are Pisces, her birthday is February 25, mine is February 24, a few years—well maybe a lot of years earlier. Chelsea does stand-up; I did stand-up. (Now I like to do sit-down.) Chelsea's comedy is out there; some say mine is too! She has written humorous books—I have written one and working on another. She really likes to drink. I'll have a couple of drinks. But, Hey, Chelsea, I've been drinking longer. She has people who call her "bitch." I call myself "old bitch." It sounds like I could easily be her BITCH AUNT.

Recently I noticed a poster at Curves. It read, "You don't stop playing because you grow old. You grow old because you stop playing." Chelsea, I want to come play with you! I don't want to climb any apple trees, but hanging out would be fun—maybe go to Cheese Cake Factory. If you think Chelsea and I could have fun together, email her at chelsea@chelseahandler.com.

21

Fun with Ghosts

We purchased our home from a widow in Roswell, Georgia. On several mornings we arose to find our seldom used, always locked, front door wide open! How could this happen?

One Saturday my youngest was downstairs in our daylight basement cleaning his room, while I was upstairs cleaning mine. All of a sudden I heard a loud noise and then "Oh no" in a deep voice. I opened the basement door and at the same time we asked each other, "Are you OK?" Our oldest son S.C was trying to put up a poster in his room of a rock music group. It kept falling off the wall even though he used lots of thumbtacks. Why??

A bit freaky—and it wasn't even Friday!

My cousin Ada Marie died at 35. She left a beautiful family: three young children, a husband, and her mother.

Side story: My Aunt Emily's husband died of a heart attack while shoveling show and she found him. She was the one with her father and, later, her mother, when they died. Then she lost her only child, Ada Marie.

While lying in bed, crying over my cousin's death, I opened my eyes in the dark room to see my grandmother's face surrounded by small clouds. My grandmother said, "Ada Marie is fine. She is with me." As quickly as she appeared, she disappeared. I have to say it shook me up.

About 20 years later Hubby and I went to a company Christmas party. We chatted with old friends Mickey and her husband from our Clearwater, Florida, days. Some friends told us they'd be having a party in about two weeks.

A few days later Hubby told me that Mickey had died in her sleep of a heart attack. She was a type A personality and a bit overweight. I'm just saying, not judging. I told Hubby, as I shed a few tears, "I guess the party is off." Then I added, "You know, Mickey would think that was really funny." Even though sad, I tend to see humor sometimes when others do not.

The following February I called Mickey's husband to see if he would like to meet my widow friend. He told me he had already met someone. Surprising, but not unusual for a happily married man. He told me they had met at a church singles group. Nine months later I called him to ask if he would come to my husband's birthday party.

At the party a goose-pimple moment happened. As our friend was introducing his lady friend, I saw the face of his dead wife surrounded by a thin layer of clouds. At the very moment I was introduced, Mickey said to me, "I like her, Emily. I hope you do too." This happened years ago, yet it still gives me goose pimples.

While Hubby was in Atlanta, I was at our then Palm Harbor cottage hanging out with the dogs and a house guest. An hour later while reading in bed, I sensed "something." I looked to my left, towards my locked bedroom door. I saw a shadowy figure of slender white clouds approximately 2 feet wide by 3 or 4 feet tall come through the unopened door. I was startled, to say the least. I had read that ghosts are unsettled spirits. In other words they have unsettled events which have kept them on earth. I said, "Go towards the light." I was relieved when the ghost traveled in a straight line and went out the window.

I enjoyed reading Phenomenon by Sylvia Brown, a bestselling author and well-known psychic, even though I had a problem with the Irish events described in the book. I don't think my odd experiences would surprise her even though they sure did SURPRISE ME.

About five years ago I had two older Dalmatians, My My and Tex. I had lost My My in April when she was 14. In October when I returned home I let Tex out. Later, I heard a bark that sounded like My My (a bit unsettling). I opened the door to call Tex and saw a little white shadow the same size and height of My My. Talk about eerie.

22

Fun with Houseboys

In some 1960s and '70s movies, we see wealthy Californians who employ adorable houseboys. Some Californians call them cabana boys. These men usually answer the door, serve food, and do whatever you need. Houseboy could be a new name for butler. California houseboys—at least in the movies—wear Hawaiian shirts and shorts.

My houseboys don't live or work full-time at our house, nor do they dress in cute outfits. They are part-time guys who do jobs on the house or in the yard. Some are really handsome; most are average looking.

As Hubby and I were finishing building our Florida home, I checked it daily. One day I was up in the bonus room talking with the contractors. Up the stairs came an adorable 30-something electrician, tall, dark hair, great big blue eyes, and a damn fine muscled body. OK, I had to say it so you'd get the picture. I was standing about three feet from the stairs when he appeared. I said to him, "Hi, I'm Emily." To the supervisor I said, "You didn't tell me he was so handsome." The electrician blushed, grinned, tripped and fell about three feet from me. I said, "I've waited all my life for a guy to fall at my feet."

Poor guy! Did I stop there? No, no, no! I told all the other workers who knew him. Unfortunately, I haven't seen him since. Fifteen years, but who's counting?

Another moment, maybe my most embarrassing, happened about the same time. I was in the backyard with an attractive landscape guy. We live in a nice community. In our subdivision the builders had put up a six-foot wooden fence along the back of the lots. Our neighbors behind us own three acres. Along with their house are a barn, a truck, and several boats. We had no problem with what they wanted to do, but we didn't like to look at our fence. I was talking to the handsome landscaper, saying, "As you can see, I need to get your advice on fast-growing bushes." At that precise moment our neighbor, well within hearing distance, pulled himself up and said, "Hi, I'm your neighbor," as he introduced himself. Talk about EMBARRASSED!

I found out from a friend of his what beer he liked. I took him a 12-pack when they had a neighborhood watch party. I introduced myself to his wife and told her I had a "kiss up" gift for her husband. I think by the time I saw him he had downed a beer or two. I said, "Here is a 'kiss up' gift for you." He said, "Great, thank you," and he started to kiss me on the lips. Luckily I moved, and he pecked my cheek. Was I ever surprised!

Another houseboy called himself "Jake." He walked with a limp. What a character! He was about 5'8", extremely thin, with a wrinkled face, in his 40s, but looked older. His clean T-shirts always had the sleeves cut off, displaying well-muscled arms.

He told me when he got out of the Navy in San Francisco, he bought a motorcycle. One moment he was sitting at a red light, the next thing he knew he was in the hospital. He had 26 operations. He always had pain. However, he was one of the most pleasant, fun-loving people I have ever met.

He owned a very rusty truck. He got me real good deals on topsoil—though he probably lost half of it through the holes in his truck! He loved to stand beside the mechanically-tuned truck and say, "We kind of look alike, don't we?"

What an inspiration! He helped me with painting and did my yard for a while. Finally he told me it was too hard on him. He was going back to driving a big truck. Sometime later I tried to contact him, but his phone was out of service. He used to drop by the house, but I haven't seen him in years. I hope God is watching over him. I miss him and that great big smile. Funny how God moves people in and out of our lives isn't it? I believe I became a better person for knowing him.

Like houseboys, most of us have worked hard during our lifetimes. Hubby grew up in Dayton, Ohio, and spent summers on his uncle's farm. My family moved to my grandparents' farm in southern Ohio when I was nine. It was my job to feed the chickens and collect the eggs. How I hated those hens! Man, can they bite! Ugly too, and they start out so adorable with cute, fluffy yellow feathers.

The job I hated most was using a putty knife to scrape dried hog poo off the floor of the hog houses. The tops were hinged to open. My dad used a hoe to break the packed poo. Where he couldn't reach, I had to use the putty knife because the hog house had to be clean for the new babies. It was a stinky, yucky job.

I had to hang clothes outside to dry, even in the winter. We didn't know what a dryer was—we're talking ancient history here. Sometimes a piece of laundry would nearly freeze before I got the next one on the clothesline. It was almost worse than cleaning the hog houses. Mother soon taught me to iron. I never minded it much . . . except the time Mother had me iron 22 of my dad's and brother's shirts. Man, was I tired!

That might be why most farm kids rarely get into trouble. They don't have time and they are exhausted. Maybe I get into so much trouble now because I'm not working as hard.

Today I'm fortunate to have service people come in occasionally to help in the house or yard. Maybe because I worked so hard all my life, I appreciate help more than most. Hey, if at times the help comes in the form of cute guys, Thank God!

23

Fun with College Dating

In the fall of 1953 I arrived at Mary Washington College and was housed off campus with a very sweet family. Unfortunately, I had to share a double bed with my roommate. If I had been worldlier I would have gone to the Dean of Woman.

My "roomie" was from a divorced family in Montgomery, Alabama. I hadn't known anyone who had divorced parents. Although not a beauty, she knew lots of stuff about make-up and bras. I resented her advice. It was difficult as she was a Southern city girl and I a Northern "country" one.

The other upstairs bedroom had twin beds with two girls from Pennsylvania. I got along better with them. One of them was a debutant. I learned about "society" and how the rich live. I hung out with a couple of dorm girls from Virginia. I wish I had kept in touch.

My Aunt Helen (mother's younger sister) and Uncle Paul lived in Culpepper, VA, 35 miles away. Sometimes Uncle Paul would come get me for a long weekend. We would jitterbug and have bubble gum blowing contests. I attended their Methodist Church and took part in the youth activities. I met a cute high school senior who came over to Fredericksburg a couple of times.

When I took the train home for Christmas vacation, I sat next to a really cute sailor, Joe, and soon we were dating. A fun guy I liked a lot, but he got too serious too soon and asked me to marry him in late spring. We broke up the following fall when I transferred to Ohio State University.

At O.S.U. I certainly had a great dorm life. I had a few dates with sweet, but rather uninteresting guys. Around Christmas time I met a pharmacy student who introduced me to two cute freshmen. They walked me home from my theater job (cashier/ candy/ popcorn sales.) They asked me to fix them up for an upcoming dance. I said, "I'll be happy to introduce you to girls, if you'll get me a date." They both were tall (6'2" and 6'4"). The taller one was a red head—the other had a dark Crew Cut and wore glasses. It was Crew Cut that asked me out. We dated off and on for four years. He was a perfect gentleman, fun, a good dancer, and <u>very</u> bright! We had a lot of very interesting, intelligent conversations.

My summer school roommate and I volunteered to be hostesses at a dance. We would go up to guys and ask them who they would like to dance with. Several times I was asked. That is where I met Fly Boy. We started dating, but we broke up after he threw a bottle in a bar. I'm not patient with bad behavior or excessive drinking.

A college friend introduced me to a cute red headed engineering student who was 6'4". I was his date for his fun fraternity sweetheart weekend. The guys moved out of the frat house and we girls moved in. The rebel raiser that I am, I organized a water balloon drop on the frat boys next door.

While some of the girls were doing their hair and nails, I taught the other the girls to hand stitch their guy's underwear so they would have a hard time getting their legs through the openings. I also short sheeted George. (You fold the top sheet over the bottom one and pull it up so it is only about three feet in length then the person can't get their feet all the way down.) I learned this trick at 4-H camp. We dated several months, but there just wasn't much chemistry there.

Soon a suite mate of mine introduced me to her engineer friend and his fraternity brothers. That is when I met a sweet guy with an adorable grin, J.C.

One Saturday I actually had three different dates in one day. Lunch with Fly Boy, an afternoon band concert with a cute, but boring, law student, and an evening date with J.C. It was fun, but too hectic for me. Most of my college dating consisted of dating Crew Cut and J.C. They were exceptional guys, very bright, caring, with good ethics, yet fun to be with. In later years one got a Phd, the other over a dozen patents. They had both worked their way through college like I had.

My senior year after J.C. graduated, I ran into some of his frat brothers. They asked if I heard from him. I said no, other than he was working in Florida. They asked if they could fix me up as they missed me at their parties. I said, "Sure." So I had a blind date with Dick and we dated for a while. A day later Bill calls and asks to go to the same frat party. I fixed him up with my girlfriend Jo. Soon they were engaged and married. Years later they look good, are active, and Bill is still working.

My final quarter at Ohio State was very busy. I worked two jobs and was taking 21 hours of classes. I still dated Crew Cut from time to time. J.C. had started writing me and flew in one weekend to see his frat brothers and me. He gave me his fraternity pin. I saw him during summer vacation when I was working in Dayton, Ohio. J.C. and I agreed to date others, but still wrote. I spent a lot of time with new girl friends and college pals, including Crew Cut when he was home. I also met a cute guy through my work, Don, who was loads of fun and had a convertible. I knew our friendship wouldn't go anywhere as he was Catholic and I didn't want a bunch of kids.

During this time I introduced my girl friend to him. They later married. If I get internet savvy I'm going to "hunt them" down.

I continued to date J.C. and Crew Cut until I married J.C. At a party on July 4th two days before our wedding I sat between them. I danced all the fast dances with Crew Cut and the slow ones with J.C. We had invited Crew Cut as we both liked him and he knew everyone coming. We had a great wedding weekend with our friends. My roommate of two years, Mary Lou, was in Key West and pregnant. Barb and Erma, my senior roommates, were my bridesmaids. All contributed to the fun. I learned a big life lesson. Don't expect all your friends to get along just because you love them.

In the fifties and early sixties, before "the pill," nice girls did not have sex before marriage. At Ohio State we did hear of some engaged girls who "put out."

The most important thing I learned from college dating? Get to know the other person really well before you marry and have kids. It will save you time, money, and your nerves. Get to know someone really well before you "do it." Hormones emitted during sex cause a woman to want to bond and love a man. This does not happen to guys. Always protect yourself.

24

Fun Flying

Sometime ago Hubby and I were on a small plane for a short flight. I chatted with a couple of middle-aged, average looking guys. They wore T-shirts with printing on the front, one guy wore glasses.

Finally, I said, "You guys have to be computer guys or engineers." They told me they worked in the computer industry. They asked me how I knew. I said, "Easy. I can see you got your clothes from Nerds R Us."

Sorry, that's just how it is. The nerd type of guy is usually a brilliant, rarely handsome guy, who more often than not can't dance or communicate well. He has a great sense of humor. He is most often a workaholic. I recognize this type of guy since I dated several in college, and I have also been married to a similar one for over fifty years. These guys tend to be loyal and down to earth types. They tend to hang out with other computer guys or engineers. Brilliant minds (male or female) have always been very interesting to me.

My husband was in a fraternity of primarily engineers. I loved those "Triangle Guys." We went back to OSU for a Triangle function several years ago—a long weekend full of various events. There were probably about fifteen or more engineers—most with their wives. At the last night's banquet, each of the guys got up and spoke about their career. Most were in their late sixties or early seventies and still working. If their wives were there, they introduced them and told how they met. One couple met in high school and the rest were blind dates. They are the Bill Gates type, not usually the guys that gals lust after. Without exception, <u>all</u> the engineers' wives I've met have been fun, bright, and very nice looking. Some of them have educated their guys in the art of wearing attractive clothing. Most of the wives buy their clothing. These guys usually prefer the old jeans or khakis and the weird T-shirts look. Although they take showers, they could care less what is covering their body.

I have to tell you a true, funny story that will illustrate this perfectly. Dateline 1967 or '68, the time for wild clothes. A lot of men wore sideburns and checkered pants. They also wore bright shirts. Hubby wore much milder clothes than some of our neighborhood guys in Metro Atlanta. I wanted my man to look sharp so I had gotten him a pair of cotton red, white, and navy checkered pants, a short-sleeved navy shirt, and a red tie. OK, it was the hippie era, so this was conservative! Normally I left the house before Hubby was out of the shower. He fixed the boys' breakfasts and saw them onto the school bus. That evening I saw him come in the door with theses pants and a medium-pink shirt, and a grey-striped tie. (How embarrassing) I explained to him that red, white, and navy goes with red, white, and navy, <u>and</u> nothing else. Soon I gave up and donated his pants to Goodwill. Thank God now he does a lot better. I am sure 99 percent of engineers' wives could tell similar, if not funnier, stories.

Traveling the skies a year ago from Kansas City to Atlanta, I upgraded to first class. I decided to live it up since I don't spend money driving out my driveway every day. (I have a 2002 van with fewer than 60,000 miles on it.) I don't spend money betting on dogs or horses. I seldom drink and eat big-ticket items, so I decided to pay $19 for an upgrade. Yes, I can rationalize almost anything.

Guess who sat next to me in first class? (I love saying that.) A really cute pilot, I jokingly said, "I would feel safe in your hands. I rate all pilots on their landings, and I seldom give A's. When I'm leaving the plane I tell pilots, "Hey, that was a B/B+/A-etc." What can they do? They just grin or laugh. Sometimes they say, "It's difficult to land a big plane." However, my young pilot seat mate told me that he had more trouble landing his small Cessna 172 than a big 747. Sometimes pilots say "It was the turbulence." Frankly, I'm just glad to get safely from one place to another.

Leaving Atlanta for Florida, I boarded a <u>small</u> plane. Inside to my left, stood the pilot, an older guy who looked bored to death. You could almost hear him thinking, *I only have 100 more of these to do before I can retire.* His name tag read "Dan."

I smiled and told him I had just come off a flight from Kansas and I gave the pilot an "A" on his landing. I asked him, "Can you do as well?" "Delta Dan" just grinned. I sat near the front, on the isle (no first class).

I asked him, maybe loudly, if he was going to dance and sing us "Up, Up, and Away."

"No, that was Eastern Airlines' song," he said. I said, "What is Delta's?" He replied, "I don't know." I then said to the other passengers near me, "Are we going to trust our lives to a pilot that doesn't even know his own airline's song?" Captain Dan finally laughed. Then I started chanting, "Captain Dan, he's our man. He can land this plane, yes he can."

Soon a lot of people joined in. We all did it again as we left the plane. At least he was smiling—even if he was on his countdown to retirement.

Today we need to make traveling as much fun as possible. While traveling I have met some really interesting people. Recently I sat next to a gal who trains tellers. She was very sweet and bright, but maybe not as fun as some of the guys.

Coming back from the Dalmatian Club of America Specialty in Kansas City, I met an engineer. Thank God I understand and like those guys. We had to sit on the runway for 2.5 hours, and then we had a 3-hour flight. I was glad I was sitting next to a bright guy. I had my notebook with me so I could have spent my time writing if I "had" to. However, for me, talking is ALWAYS more fun than writing.

When I asked him what he did, he said he was employed by the La Sal Company.

I said, "That's the company that makes dairy equipment?" He was stunned, and asked me how I knew that. I said, "My grandparents had a dairy."

I love to shock and <u>maybe</u> impress bright guys. He went on to tell me about his job. HINT to young, sweet, single gals: If you want an engineer to talk to you, ask them lots of questions about their work. These guys are ready to talk. You just have to ask the right questions. The same probably applies to most guys.

As we talked I asked him if he had read *The Tipping Point.* He said, "No." I teased, "Well, if I had been interviewing you, I probably wouldn't have hired you."

Stunned him again. He asked about the book. A company grows and grows and then becomes number one. However, no company, current example is Toyota, can maintain that spot, it's just not possible. He said he was going to read it.

As we sat on the runway in Kansas City because of the storm in Atlanta, this guy calls his wife several times. I spent about five hours with him before we finally reached Atlanta. He would have a three-hour lay over. I had two hours, so I asked him if he would like to join me for dinner at Paschal's Restaurant. They have two there, one is a small café/cafeteria. The other is larger and much more of a relaxing atmosphere.

The engineer called his wife. I said, "I want to talk to her." I say, "Hi, I'm the bitch who sat next to your husband for hours. I'm seventy-five, but I'm still a hottie." We both laughed as I handed him the phone. After we ate, I asked, "Are you going to walk me to my gate?" He said, "Sure."

While I ran into the restroom he heard my flight being called. When I came out, he told me that he had run down to the gate and told them I was on my way. I had no problem making my plane. But wasn't that sweet of him? I meet so many interesting people, don't I?

On the plane for Florida I was seated next to a thirty-something cutie who is also an author. We talked about his book, and I read him a chapter of mine. He said he was going to get it for his wife and wanted to read it, too. WOW! I didn't plan this to be a book a guy might like. Life is full of surprises, isn't it? He also told me how much he loves his wife and kids. Very refreshing, isn't it?

25

Fun Going to Europe with J.D.

Have you seen the wonderful movie, *The Bucket List*, starring Jack Nicholson and Morgan Freeman? If not, do. It will make you think about your life.

On the top of my bucket list was a trip to the south of France. Hubby said it wasn't on his bucket list, so I asked our 26-year-old grandson, J.D. In August 2009 we were to meet in Atlanta and fly to Paris, change planes, and fly to Barcelona. Then take a taxi to the cruise ship a few miles away.

Hubby and I left North Carolina in plenty of time. We were waiting for J.D. at the baggage area. I had a bad cold and was "a bit out of it."

J.D. finally called us when he was boarding the plane. I rushed to check in. Air France was weighing everyone's luggage, the line was long, so I missed my plane. Air France put me on a Delta flight that was to leave TWO hours later, with a TWO-hour layover in Paris. It cost an extra $200. OUCH! I remembered later that J.D. said he'd meet me at the gate. Damn! Hubby helped me check in and then I was on my own. Luckily I got a hold of J.D.

Actually, I had a great time waiting, as I went to the bar for food and a drink. I had lunch with two guys and a gal. Soon it was time to board. Note: Life is what you make it. Have fun. Talk to people.

The trip was rough, I was not feeling well, and couldn't sleep even with Ambien. As usual I was lugging too much stuff: one large 59-lb. suitcase, a carry-on, a heavy tote bag, a large poncho, and a big sweater. I had to manage all that stuff in Paris and Barcelona. Finding my way around in both cities without speaking French or Spanish was interesting.

Flying to Paris, I sat next to a guy from Atlanta. He helped me with my carry-on. My fun seat mate, who worked in the medical field, was en route to Stockholm. After dinner he removed long flannel pj's from his carry-on and went into the restroom to change. He also put on long, black support socks to help with blood circulation. My ankles did swell though I got up often. I bought socks like his for the return trip and did a lot better. Talking with my seat mate made the long trip fun.

Finally, finally, finally, I made it to the large ship, the Royal Caribbean's *Voyager of the Seas*. How would I find J.D. in that crowd? But there he was standing on board, ready for the safety drill.

We had reserved assigned seating for dinner. Most of the passengers were Caucasian, some Spanish, a good many English, a few French, very few Americans and some were African American. J.D. and I were seated at an eight-top table with six other people, all African American. It was strange to be in the minority. "Are y'all kin, or did you all go to the same tanning bed?" I said. Fortunately, they thought it was funny. They were from Philadelphia and Baltimore. The parents had been educators. Their two well educated daughters had paid for their trip. My grandson and I really looked forward to our dinners with them. The last evening, I asked them if they would adopt us and let us be their "albino relatives."

J.D. and I met an interesting, handsome international couple with a teenage son. She was from Tucson, he from England. The couple first met in Hawaii. The family was living in Saudi Arabia, where the father was in the construction business. They own a house in Spain.

We also met a British couple from Birmingham, England. Denise is a beautiful flight attendant working for British Airways. She has two adult sons. Steve had his teenage girls with them. I told Denise, in front of Steve, that even though he was "sort of cute," she could do better. The more you tease the English lads, the more they seem to like it. Steve told me he wished they had met me earlier in the trip. I told him it wouldn't have done any good . . . I still thought Denise could do better.

We left Barcelona before dawn and arrived back in Atlanta about 10 hours later. Hubby was waiting, thank God. It was a typical HOT Atlanta day. Hubby couldn't find his car, which had never happened before. That was NOT fun! I had a REAL HARD time not bitching. By the time I got back home and into bed, I had gone an exhausting 26 hours without sleep.

J.D. could not have been a more wonderful traveling buddy. When I asked him what he liked best on the trip, he said, "All of it!" He sent us a lovely thank-you note.

J.D.'s mannerisms remind me so much of my Hubby. This SHOULD NOT surprise me, as I have often seen this genetic pattern in my dogs. He seems to have more fun than his granddad, and is becoming a wonderful man. Thank you, God!

26

Fun Losing Weight

Losing weight and becoming healthy can be fun if you have the right attitude. How? Join a support group like TOPS (Take Off Pounds Sensibly) or Weight Watchers. Both can get you results if you're motivated, weigh in, and attend the weekly meetings. I prefer TOPS since it costs a lot less money and there is more interaction between members—thus, more fun. The experts say we need exercise too. Ugh. I go to Curves three times a week for 30 minutes, which is "doable." You can talk and have fun. If I go three times a week and have no more than two desserts, I lose weight or keep stable. It's that simple. Curves has a sign that reads: SUCCESS FEELS GREAT. NOW I CAN FILL MY CLOSET WITH CLOTHES THAT AREN'T BLACK!

Originally I started going to Curves to build up muscle around my knees. Two orthopedic doctors told me that for every pound you take off, it takes four pounds of pressure off your knees. I had tried physical therapy and found it very boring and painful. I saw it as an appointment for pain.

So, to save money, I signed up at Curves for a whole year. I'm in my seventh year. I feel so much better, so it's worth it!

Other benefits of working out, besides feeling better, is losing weight and looking better in clothes. I have gone down nearly four sizes. Not too shabby for someone who doesn't work out that hard. I saw a big difference in my stress test results. I lost both of my parents because of heart problems.

Both of my younger siblings are on heart medications. I am not. My blood pressure, pulse, etc., are healthy. My doctor is happy with my numbers, but would be happier if I lost 20 more pounds. Me too. People say I look and act younger. I feel it is exercise, attitude, and trying to eat healthily. Not easy, but worth it in the long run.

I started going to TOPS when my weight reached a plateau and I felt I needed to be held accountable. Every week I learn something new. Still, losing and keeping weight off is VERY difficult.

In Florida, my friends Loretta and Sandy weigh us in every week. Loretta recently gave us slips of paper marked with the weight we lost during the last year. Some of the women had lost BIG TIME, as much as 46 pounds. I like to think I helped inspire them since I led most of the programs.

Guess what I lost? You won't believe it, less than three pounds. With that revelation I made fun of myself as we giggled. The next week we had an even bigger laugh. Every week when our name is called, we tell whether we lost or gained. We don't usually say how much we have gained, but do say what we lose. I lost 3 pounds and tied for "Best Loser of the Week." This is a big deal: you get a trophy for a week and a dollar. Then everyone stands up and sings to you! OK, you skinny-Minnie girls, you would never win it. When I bragged and said "3 pounds," my smartass friend, Karen, remarked, "Gee, Emily, that's more than you lost all last year!" We all laughed! I'm sure she wouldn't do that to anyone else. I loved it! Another side benefit from TOPS and Curves is making new friends.

Check out what you know, with this test. Good news, I give you the answers before I give you the questions.

1. True—I heard of this guy, Bill Heidel, who went from 535 to 165 pounds in two years. He did it by asking himself if he really wanted whatever food it was, or would he rather be slender and healthy.
2. False—The "chocolate diet": You don't eat anything but chocolate. How's that for a fun but unwise idea? Don't we wish, wish, wish we could lose weight that way?
3. True—If hunger is sudden, it is caused by stress or lack of water. This is especially true if you're hungry for sweet or salty items. (Sometimes the body doesn't know whether it's hunger or thirst.)

Try a glass of water first, wait 20 minutes, and then have 10-12 almonds, eaten slowly, and drink a glass of water.

4. False—Buy a bathing suit two sizes too small and stop eating until you fit into it. Sure, but you could die in the process.
5. True—Become accountable with a diet partner or group.
6. True—Every time you feel like eating, grab your partner and have sex. Yeah sure, especially with a lot of people around?
7. True—Resolve to get healthy. Treating your body right by eating more raw fruits and vegetables.
8. True—Instead of eating, jump rope in the nude . . . preferably in front of a mirror. Jumping rope and dancing are excellent forms of exercise, but do eat properly.
9. True—After hours of fasting and sleeping, your body needs fuel. Eat a good breakfast. No time? Have a Slim-Fast bar or shake, or a banana with peanut butter on a whole wheat bun, as Dr. Oz suggests.
10. True—Take a really good vitamin every day. I like Life's Fortune. It's made of green food.
11. True—Dr. Phil says, "You can get real about fat or you can get real fat."
12. False—The "toilet diet": Drink 40 glasses of water a day while cleaning your bathroom. No, don't drink more than 10 to 12, or you will mess up your electrolytes. Eight, however, is really good for your skin, digestion, kidneys, and bladder as it helps remove fat from your body. Cleaning your bathroom is good anytime. Housecleaning is good too, except if I have to do it!
13. True—Give up sugar and you will not only feel a lot better, you will lose weight. Sugar is like a drug, you eat a little and you want more. When Ellen DeGeneres gave up sugar she claimed she had a great deal more energy.
14. True—Watching TV uses energy. Well, maybe some, but a lot more if you lift weights during commercials. Set a good example for your children.
15. False—The "cake diet": Eat all you want and become lumpity-dumpity. Not good.
16. True—Set goals that are obtainable, such as five pounds a month. If you say, "I am going to lose 150 pounds this year," it just seems too difficult.

17. True—If you get hungry in the middle of the night, have a cracker by your bed to avoid the kitchen.
18. True—Use a smaller plate and serve food from the kitchen. Seconds easily available are not a good thing.
19. True—VERY IMPORTANT! Eat slowly and enjoy every bite! Try chewing every bite 20 times.
20. True—If you don't watch your curves, no one else will either. People are simply attracted to healthy, young-looking bodies. Take care of what God gave you.

Discuss a realistic weight with your doctor. According to Dr. Phil, you need to get rid of your fat clothes NOW. I have found that clothes even one size too large can make me look fatter. Think "green" and consider resale shops. Sometimes they have really neat designer clothes.

Go to a major department store for a makeup makeover. You are not required to buy. Then treat yourself with a really good haircut and a new style. Don't get caught in a "time warp"; stay sharp and up to date. Think long and hard before you "go gray." Hair color is not that hard to do and it will keep you looking younger.

Take up a new hobby and make new friends as you slim down and become a new, improved, healthier you.

Today is the beginning of the rest of your life, right? Making one healthy choice. Maybe to drink 8 glasses of water a day. It will become a habit after a month. If you make one small change every month or so you could produce BIG health benefits and improve your quality of life? It's up to you.

27

Fun on the Go

By now you realize I like to have fun. Let me tell you, one of the easiest ways is "messing" with guys. "Messing" means joking around and having innocent fun. You may not realize it, but I get bored easily. When that happens, the fun starts. This is especially true if I have to wait in line.

On Paradise Island we have a small post office with three people taking care of us. So, yes, we often have to wait. Years ago I started teasing one of the guys. I called him "The Hunk," of course loud enough for others to hear, and he laughed. I said, "Isn't he cute when he blushes." He and the other employees loved it. He is a fun guy who always seems glad to see me. I recently asked him when he went from "hunk" to "hulk."

The other day I saw him from a distance in the post office. I said, "Hey, have you got a new perm?" He said, "This is my regular hair." I said, "Sure," as I teased him. He came up to talk with me. When I told him I had a joke for him, he motioned me to another door.

(Maybe you haven't heard this one that a friend told me.)

This guy goes into a bar and sees this beautiful redhead with big blue eyes. He orders his drink. He continues to watch her. She is with a girlfriend. Her friend leaves, but he is still unable to say anything. Then all at once one of her blue eyes pops out. He ends up catching it. When he returns it to her she says, "Thank you so much! I am so glad it didn't fall on the floor." Then she asks him if he would be her guest in the dining room for a meal. They have a wonderful time. They loved the same books, movies, etc. After dinner she says, "Would you like to follow me back to my house for a cup of coffee, and breakfast?" He is delighted. They have a great time. In the morning she fixes him a delicious gourmet breakfast. He turns to her and says, "You are so beautiful, smart and fun, but why me?" She says, "You kind of caught my eye."

Don't you just LOVE it?

I was telling some of my friends at TOPS (Take Off Pounds Sensibly) that I have so much fun at the post office. They asked what post office, so I told them. They said they never have fun there. I said you can have fun anywhere—if you make your own fun.

One day I noticed this really tall, healthy-looking big guy wearing a red Hawaiian shirt. Of course, loud enough for others to hear, I said, "Great shirt, big guy!" He said, "Thanks." It made my day! It takes so little to make me happy. A cute guy who blushes does it every time—even ones who aren't so cute.

One day, "Tex" (my very handsome Champion Dalmatian) jumped on the fence and knocked some boards off. I called my neighbors to see if it was OK if I came over to survey the damage. My neighbor's brother was house sitting. He told me he would meet me at the fence. What a neat 30 something hottie he was. He insisted on fixing the fence himself, sweet guy that he is. A few years ago we both were invited to a wedding reception across the street. He was dressed up and really looked nice. After I told someone at the party I was hottie's first, he explained that I was his first yard client.

One of the older guys (80+) I enjoy is Durham. I met him while at the hospital getting blood tests, when I decided that day to thank all the volunteers. (Some were shocked!) I had to wait a while, so I got to talking with Durham. He looked sad. I asked him, "Are you married?" He told me, "I was, for 62 years. However my wife died two years ago." I said, "Are you dating anyone?" He said, "No." I said, "I have just the girl for you, she is as beautiful on the inside as she is on the outside." I also told him she was a Presbyterian.

A much younger guy next to me said, "Who is it? I go to the Presbyterian Church." I told him. He told Durham she is a nice pretty lady. Durham is a handsome guy with great big blue eyes and snow-white hair. He told me he used to be an executive for K-Mart and that he and his wife lived in North Carolina and went to a Presbyterian church. I told him Maye was from Charlotte.

I told Durham that Maye doesn't want to have sex anymore and if that was a problem, I knew another gal. He laughed. I think I made his day, even if nothing happened. I gave him her phone number and asked him to have her call me after she spoke to him.

As soon as I got home I called her. She laughed and said he probably wouldn't call. But he did. She told a mutual friend about it. Maye said, "Can you believe what Emily has done now?"

Soon I got a call from Maye. Meeting for dinner, we sat in a large booth; Maye and I on one side, Durham opposite us. We were having fun chatting when our mutual friend came over to our table. She pushed me over so she could sit down. I introduced her to Durham. The first words out of her mouth were, "Durham, did Emily tell you that Maye doesn't want to have sex?" Yes, she had both of them blushing. Then she said, "I told Maye that when you kiss her, she should stick her tongue halfway down your throat." In spite of being embarrassed, it wasn't long before they were dating. Sometimes I do nice things—but don't count on it.

My widow friend, Viv, 85, would like to start dating. I suggested she ask the local funeral director for referrals, or maybe volunteer at the hospital where she could meet some retired guys, or watch the obits and start hanging out at funerals.

Kinda reminds me of that old '80s movie, *Harold and Maude*, with the 17-year-old hooking up with the 80-year-old. I loved it! Maybe you would too.

28

Fun in France

Ah, Paris in the springtime . . . and in the summer. Don't you love it? However, I love the south of France more. I feel at home there even though I can't speak French. I have been to Paris on several short visits. Years ago we had a rude waiter, otherwise, <u>all</u> my experiences in France have been—*marvelous*! If you expect good in life, usually you get it.

You may have heard that the French are proud people. Why do you think that is? My theory goes like this: Many wars have been fought over their land. Why? They are blessed with a good climate, fertile soil, rich history, and spectacular beauty. Recall the scenery you passed through when riding along with Lance Armstrong on the Tour de France. Think of movies filmed in Paris and France, the lovely impressionist paintings, French fashions, their *ooh-la-la* perfume. Marvel at the longevity of French furniture, their fabulous food, superior wine, and their music (the classics, '40s jazz, and today's music)! The French have a sexy language and a relaxed lifestyle. Can you see they have something to be proud of?

Have you seen the movies, *Gigi*, *I Love Paris in the Springtime*, or *To Catch a Thief* (filmed in the south of France)? If you haven't seen these movies or traveled in France, you probably think all I say here is too good to be true. You need to experience France to enjoy everything there, my friend.

The French people always say "*Bonjour*" before saying anything else. "Good day"—what could be more cheerful? You'll find they react better to you if you do the same. A smile and a few manners go a long way there. After saying "*Bonjour*," I say, "I'm sorry, do you speak English?" Most people can speak basic English and understand you if you speak slowly, not loudly. (I've discovered that when asking for directions in any foreign place, it helps to go to the security people, or police.) Don't forget to say "Merci," which is "thank you" in French.

After I arrived in Paris, I had a long-distance gate change, lots of luggage, and over two hours of wait time. All I wanted was a good bed. Instead I bought a diet cola and something to eat. I was tired of reading. What to do? . . . I hate very few things, but I hate boredom. I amused myself by trying to figure out which women were French. In the summer of 2009, I noticed a lot of flax color as well as the all-white look and the usual black. They carried red or yellow handbags for a "pop" of color. One of the more attractive women wore flax and carried a yellow bag. Later on she ended up sitting on a bench near me.

While we were sitting there reading, all of a sudden two young men (about eight feet away) started yelling in French. The larger man was hitting the smaller one. Two women, probably the man's mother and his wife, tried to pull the big guy off the smaller one. All at once, two French policemen were pulling them apart.

I said to the woman next to me, "Wow, I've never seen anything like that."

She said, "Neither have I."

We listened, and then I asked her what was going on. She told me that the smaller guy had stepped on the big guy's mama's foot. The policeman made the smaller guy apologize to the lady. The big guy was still upset. The police told the offender to go on his way. They stayed with the big guy until he calmed down.

I said to the lady sitting near me, "Are you French?"

She said, "Yes."

I said, "I saw you earlier and decided you were, because you are so beautifully dressed."

She smiled. Did I help make her day? I hope so.

Then I complimented her on how well she spoke English. She asked where I was from. (I was dressed in black to blend in and because black doesn't show "traveling dirt.") I told her I was from the U.S.A. We had a pleasant conversation. She appeared to be in her late 40s, married, and had three boys. She visited our country a few years ago to see her sister in New Jersey. They traveled to New York, Chicago, and San Francisco. I was holding up, but very tired. On to Barcelona and the ship to meet up with grandson J.D.

Our first port stop in France was at Marseille on the Mediterranean Sea. They had cleaned it up since I had been there. J.D. said he could live there. After reading about "the winds" that suddenly come (*My Life in France* by Julia Child), I have my doubts. I prefer the smaller country towns, like Cassis. This small resort town, in the Provence-Alps-Côte d'Azur region is in southern France. It is located on a beautiful lake surrounded by vineyards, northeast of Marseille.

J.D. and I liked the views from the highest cliffs, but really loved Cassis. It reminded us of towns in California, as we rode around in a small open bus and saw well-kept colorful tile roofed houses and apartments. We had a cool drink and then went on to shopping. We found a lovely flax apron with rose trim for S.C.'s wife, and a provincial yellow-and-blue round tablecloth for my Florida kitchen table. In another shop we bought J.D. a shirt.

The next day we went to Nice and Monaco. We enjoyed the hour's drive along the picturesque French Riviera as we thought of Grace Kelly and Cary Grant in *To Catch a Thief*. It looks beautiful just like that with the pastel houses and condos covering the hills! Winding roads stretch from the hilltops to the sea. Everywhere you see tall palms and gorgeous trees, lush green foliage, and every color of flowers. The combination is breathtaking and we felt like we were in a movie.

As we got off the bus I asked Ms. Tour Director if she would like to join J.D. and me for a cup of coffee. There are few public restrooms in Europe, You have to order something in a restaurant in order to use theirs.

As we were chatting, she told us we were near the Nice Flower Market. It was INCREDIBLE! The 30 feet long tables displayed endless arrays of bright fruits, vegetables, and fresh fish, eggs, art booths, local ceramics, and the most marvelous flowers we had ever seen. The dew-kissed blooms were of white, ivory, pink, rose, red, and various shades of yellow and orange. I said, "*Bonjour*" to several vendors and told them their flowers were magnificent. Most spoke some English, and were charming. The floral aroma was so wonderful. I really thought I had died and gone to heaven. (If this is what heaven is like, I'm going to try really hard to get in.) This was definitely one of the high points of our trip!

I talked to an older artist for about 10 minutes while J.D. was taking photos. The artist told me he had traveled around the U.S., would love to return here, but was battling cancer. I told him I was a cancer survivor since 1985; hopefully I encouraged him.

On to marvelous Monaco, where they also speak French. Flowering shrubs of all colors bordered the streets. The carefully manicured lawns with tall palm trees were everywhere and so lovely! We found an open-air but shady café behind The Palace. What fun I had with the waiter! We started with "*Bonjour*." When I said to J.D., "He is an *ooh-la-la* waiter because he is so cute." Of course he heard me and loved it! Yes, he was fun, personable, and surprise, surprise, surprise, he gave us good service. We had paid $90 for our similar meals in Florence, and $42 in Monaco. In both cases we looked at their display board before sitting down. We got smart in Monaco and ordered a chilled carafe of water. Less costly than bottled water, colas, or wine.

After a leisurely lunch, J.D. and I visited a park where he took many photos. I sat on a bench and rested. A young couple was sitting nearby with their adorable, blue-eyed, three-year-old blonde little girl. The man could speak a little English. We talked about his very active daughter. They were French tourists who were there with another couple having a picnic lunch.

J.D. and I looked around the gift shop before boarding our bus to return to the ship. Since most companies close down in August we experienced BIG crowds everywhere!

We arrived back on the boat in time for dinner. We couldn't wait to share our adventures with our fun dinner partners. I told them, "I think Italy is beautiful, but France definitely has my heart." I was so very reluctant to leave France. I don't know why, but I feel at home there.

It would be so cool to rent a place in the South of France for our entire family. Son T.J. does quite well driving in Europe or we could take cabs. However, with all of us having very busy lives it would be difficult to schedule. Plus it would cost a lot of money. Money can buy happiness as J.D. and I found out in the South of France.

29

Fun Love Letters to Funny Celebs

Just as I have many "best friends," I have many fun and funny people I love Hey, sometimes I want my Letterman "fix" and sometimes Leno. Actually I understand that Dave and I share Midwestern backgrounds as well as an appreciation of Ruth Lyons, a 50's Cincinnati TV star (whom I had hoped to replace). I love Dave's Mom too!

Who doesn't love cutie, funny, Jimmy Fallon? I call him crazy because for a week he did the "Live with Regis and Kelly" in the morning, and then flew to California to do his own show. Afterwards taking the "red eye" back to NY to do it all over again. Crazy!

Kelly Ripa, you are America's sweetheart and oh so funny—love you. I never thought you would be able to hold your own with Regis. Well girlfriend, you proved there is always room for another strong funny gal.

Regis, Regis, Regis what are we going to do without our morning "fix" of you and Kelly? No one can fill your shoes! You are sometimes the funniest when you don't even know it. Maybe you could go on the road with Rickles and bill yourselves as "The Bad Old Boys". We need to keep seeing you!

Crazy Ferguson, you and I share getting "the mike" cut off when trying to do stand up. You are just so damn creative with your low budget show. Love you!

Ellen DeGeneres, you can really out dance me. I love your sense of humor and seemingly, effortless interviews.

Joy Behar, I like you on the "View", but love you on your show. That's a lot of pressure doing ten shows a week; let alone keeping your hair red!

Whoopee, love how you keep everyone centered on the "View." Funny lady and most of the time your remarks seem right on target. But what do I know?

Carol Burnett, I remember loving you on "The Gary Moore Show" long before you worked with funny, cutie, Vickie Laurence and your funny sidekicks. Miss all of you! Did you learn your funny stuff from "I Love Lucy"?

Don Rickles, I'm glad I sometimes get to see you on one of the talk shows. People think that I'm a female version of you. What could they be thinking?

Bonnie Hunt, we miss you on TV and in the movies. Hearing your voice in "Cars" just isn't the same as seeing you. Miss your adorable Mom too!

Kathy Griffin, your "bit" about "the wedding" killed me. Know "The Queen" loves you too, girlfriend! Just saw you on Joan Rivers' "Fashion Police." I wish I could have been on with the two of you. How Funny!

Brett Butler, the blue collar star of "Grace under Fire", I always loved you, best friend or not. About twenty years ago when you did stand-up in Atlanta, my girlfriend, Elsie, and I met you after your performance and I gave you a gift. It was a red Tee shirt with a Dalmatian and a fire truck that I had designed. You sent me a sweet handwritten note informing me that the tee had no design. Not sure what happened—embarrassing but funny. I've moved three times since that happened but I'll look to see if I have another one. I saw your movie "Bruno," and loved your performance as an old fashioned nun spelling teacher, to a young cross-dresser. Wish you would make more movies as you are such a delightful comedian, and of course, my best friend. Right?

Roseanne Barr, you have always been a beloved trailblazer from your first appearance on the Johnny Carson Show. After years of missing you, I see you looking fabulous on the David Letterman Show. I recently saw your reality show, "Roseanne's Nuts"—very interesting. I use a macadamia nut deep hair repair that I love. I also remember a macadamia nut pie that my Aunt Emily made. Damn, she would die.

Betty White, I have loved you since your earliest TV appearances. Maybe I could do a "walk on" as your bad ass cousin in "Hot In Cleveland", or maybe not!

Wanda Sikes, I would love to meet you. You are so fresh and so funny.

Tom Hanks, I have loved all your performances. I just saw you with Julia Roberts in "Larry Crowne" what fun!

Julia Roberts, I love you in anything, but girlfriend you really shine in comedies. I hope you'll consider doing a lot more of them.

I loved Jack Lemon in his comedy roles! I guess he felt he had to prove himself as a serious actor in that alcoholic role. It is not easy to make people laugh, but if you have the gift, shouldn't you use it? Don't we need more laughter in our lives!

Watch the comedy channel and you hear the f-word a lot. I don't have a problem with it once in awhile but I do feel some comedians rely on it too much. But again, what do I know?

The younger comedians to watch are those on "Saturday Night live". Like funny Seth Thomas and cutie Amy Poehler (also on "Parks and Recreation)". She looks and acts like a younger version of my friend Judy Stroup.

Melissa McCarthy cracks me up in "Mike and Lucy" but I tell everyone to see her with her husband in "Bridesmaids." Girlfriend you nailed that part!

How about Tina Frey, now a best selling author and award winning comic. I love your show "30 Rock" WOW! Tina, you get to do it with the fun, funny guys Alex Baldwin and Tracy Morgan.

Rita Rudner, you cutie you, I have loved you since your early TV years when you started "bashing guys "on the Tonight Show. Now I hear you are married, have a little girl, writing lots of books and doing stand-up in Vegas. WOW! I would love to see your act and meet you!

Two of my very, very favorites and of course best friends, that I haven't met yet, are Kathy Lee Gifford and Hoda Kotb. They are the stars of the last hour of the "Today" show. It is sad that we don't get that hour in North Carolina. These two gals along with younger sidekick, Sara, are a riot! Love, Love, Love Kathy Lee and Hoda when they are on with Jay Leno. Leno should put them in his act. I would pay for that! But I would rather join in and be a part of the party.

Kathy Lee I grew up watching you. Lie, Lie Lie. I have loved you from your "la, la" days on "Name That Tune". Loved you with Regis but honestly love, love, love, you and Hoda together. You two should put out a "Highlights" DVD of your funniest moments. Frankly—if I loved you anymore I would have to be your Momma. And aren't you glad I'm not!

30

Fun Being a Bitch

A "Bitch" is a female dog, a woman acting badly or can be a term of empowerment. Have you heard the song "Bitch" by Meredith Brooks?

My girl friend Cheryl told me "You are the best good old bitch I ever met." We both broke out in gales of laughter. Yes, I can take it as well as give it out. In fact I get real disappointed if old friends don't give it back. Some folks get "old quickly." Just because you have a history with someone doesn't mean you HAVE to have a future. Life is too short to put up with people who live in the past or aren't fun. Make a point to live in the now.

Since age 60, I've found I can get by with almost anything short of murder. I love to verbally shock people. I live to put a smile on people's faces. I believe God wants us to have fun. When someone asks me how I am? I say, "Fine for an old bitch." The judgmental types act like they don't hear me. They are probably saying, "God give me a break, I don't need this." Most younger people and men LOVE IT. If you would rather be known as an "old biddy," fine. However, after four near death experiences, I just want to be known as a good, positive, fun person.

Some of my girlfriends are really good at getting me back. TRUE GIRLFRIENDS ARE THE MOST WONDERFUL GIFTS GOD GIVES US. Ok, Hubby and family, you are expected to love me—girlfriends choose to! A true girl friend is ALWAYS there for you. She checks on you if she hasn't heard from you for awhile.

Question: Does a true girl friend tell her girl friend that her husband/boyfriend is running around? She may tell *him* in person, email, or text that he had better get his act together or he may lose the best thing in his life. I believe a true friend is very careful not to tell her friend that she thinks he is the lowest creature in the universe, even if they are divorcing. They could get back together. You don't want to ruin your friendship with her.

Beware, or you'll become a bitchy witch. Quite a few years ago two former close dog show people, whom I thought were friends, proved they were true bitchy witches. Jealousy is a horrible thing. Now both of these people have less than great lives. Thank God I'm not a jealous person.

As someone wise said, "What goes around comes around." If you have read, *The Secret* by Rhonda Byrne, you know this is true. You choose to be a positive or negative person.

There are some bitchy witches that could benefit from a new operation, an iserectomy. A hospital volunteer told me about this surgery. The doctor cuts the cord from the brain to the asshole. The benefit—it allows "assholes" to become normal people. This is a joke. Did I "get ya?"

At times things seem bad or unfair, but if you honestly try to be a good person—admit when you are wrong (and we all are at times) good things usually happen. I always have wondered why some people have such a hard time saying "I'm sorry" or even "Thank you."

Sometimes I open my big mouth and hurt a friend unintentionally. When I realize I have, I do apologize. Then I pray for forgiveness—and forgive myself. NO ONE IS PERFECT! But I do believe God wants us to be happy. However sometimes friends don't forgive you. Move on as you both make new friends.

I think we all need to keep on making new friends in life. You lose friends, some die before you know it, or move away. Open your heart to people of all ages. I love my young friends for their fresh outlook on life, their energy and ability to have fun. I love my older friends for their surprising insight, bright remarks, and sometimes funny, twisted look at life. They are like ripe fruit—full and delicious.

Someone asked me how I could have so many friends. You have to go the extra mile to develop new friendships. You need to email, call, and/or write notes. You have to write more than one line on Christmas cards.

When friends need you, you have to try to be there for them. If you see a small gift, cartoon, or magazine article they might like, drop it in the mail. Overlook their faults if you expect them to overlook yours. To have friends you have to be a good one.

This came from a card, author unknown.

> Girlfriends stick together
> Through thick and thin
> Through up and down
> Through fat and skinny
> Through young and old
> Through good and bad
> Through hot and cold . . .
> How lucky I am to have a friend like you! Thank you for all you do, for who you are, for bringing out the best in me!

Cherish your friends and loved ones before God needs them.

31

Fun in Italy

My grandson J.D. spent his senior year at an interesting international school in Lanciano, Italy, on the Adriatic Coast. He had lots of fun seeing the sights on class excursions. (Rome, Florence, and Venice.)

After his graduation, our family rented rooms in a lovely old Italian farmhouse—taking many day trips. The rolling hills covered with vineyards were beautiful! The small towns where we stopped to see the sights and have lunch were a joy. The people were very sweet. The history there is something that needs to be experienced. Who wouldn't have fun in Italy?

Though I appreciate the antiquity and architecture of Rome, I prefer the Italian countryside. I stayed on ship and rested as J.D. took the tour to see Rome again. I had a manicure and a session with the acupuncturist (trained in China.) Afterwards I did feel much better.

The next day grandson and I decided to take the cruise bus to Florence. He had been there before, but I had not. Walking on miles of cobblestones was very tiring. I thought I must be getting old, as it seemed so hot that day. With low blood pressure, heat doesn't usually bother me. We found out it was 107° Fahrenheit.

We met a gal from Northwest Canada who was traveling with her sister. She had heard me tell J.D. I wasn't up to walking around Pompeii in the heat, so she joined me. We had fun chatting and enjoying frozen lemonade slushies.

We had a better trip to Naples and Capri eight years before when J.D.'s dad hired us a driver with a large golf cart. The streets are extremely narrow and crowded with tourists. When we went before in late May, the crowds weren't as bad. We also had more time to enjoy the sights.

This time, everyone on our ship waited for two hours before we were allowed off. We found out later that Italian government and doctors were inspecting the ship's medical records. The rumor was that on the ship's last trip, 40 crew members had been ill. We were told the ship had been thoroughly cleaned. Fortunately, no one I heard of got sick this time. This did shorten our time in the area.

Our bus wound through the streets of Naples as we heard about the city's fascinating history. Then we, with about 100 others, boarded a large motorboat for a pleasant cruise to Capri. In Capri, we took a long trek over cobblestones, only to stand in a crowd in the heat for an hour. Not fun! At the mountain's top we found the expected photo op of a scenic view, some shops, and a stand that sold soft drinks and slushies. I had a lemonade slushy while I waited for grandson as he explored and took pictures.

We ran into our international friends we had met at breakfast. They were so sweet to me, as they helped me on and off the lift. Sometimes I forget that I'm not 40.

From the motorboat, we boarded a bus that took us on a picturesque and restful coastal drive on our way to Sorrento. The high cliffs were filled with quaint colorful houses overlooking the rugged coast. The blue sky and backdrop of the Mediterranean Sea make you aware you are in a special place. No wonder movie stars love to spend time there. The crowded beaches are like none I had ever seen; instead of sand, there are black stones ranging in size from two to six inches. Yet the beach attracts a multitude of sunbathers, some of them topless.

Our group had lunch at an absolutely magnificent restaurant. I am sure I had seen photos of the outside area in one of my decorating magazines. Picture this: A stucco wall with Bougainvillea flowers trailing over it, an arched wrought-iron gate with a stone entrance, and a patio. The restaurant was surrounded on two sides by arbors draped with ancient grapevines, the trunks eight to ten inches wide. Next to the arbors were narrow gardens of lemon trees with giant lemons (3" X 5") and flowers of all colors. Lovely bouquets were placed on white linen draped tables.

Soon, large chilled bottles of water, white wine, and bread were delivered as J.D. and I sat with our new friends. Then a fragrant plate of Italian pasta and tomato sauce and cheese was set in front of each of us. Unfortunately, I'm allergic to all of it. So I simply said "No thank you." It wasn't three minutes before the manager, the headwaiter, and the waitress were asking what they could get me. I said, "If it is not too much trouble, I would like a house salad." They asked if I would like it with grilled chicken. I said, "No thank you, I'm also allergic to chicken." (It isn't easy being me.) I tried not to be a pain. This is difficult when you know you are being a pain.

I can't begin to tell you how extraordinary this luncheon was to us. We felt it was so special to be in such a beautiful place enjoying our meal and wine. Truly one of the trip's highlights! Unfortunately, it was over too quickly. Riding along the scenic coast we had time to reflect on this unforgettable experience.

32

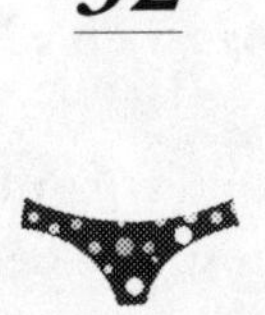

Fun Reducing Stress

When you reduce your stress level you WILL have more fun.

1. Get seven or more hours of sleep.
2. Eat plenty of fruits and vegetables.
3. Send out more smiles and joy and you'll get more in return.
4. Try not to complain or be judgmental.
5. Allow others to teach you about life.
6. Keep your doctor check-ups. Check out any pain. Maybe you'll find, like I did, it wasn't cancer, just arthritis.
7. Try natural healings such as a chiropractors and acupuncturist. Seek recommendations from others.
8. It is better to ask someone for help than to complain.
9. Laugh as much as possible.
10. Take deep breaths to calming music.
11. Get lost in a repetitive activity like knitting, dancing or exercise.
12. Concentrate on the water as you shower.
13. Massage your forehead, temples, jaw, and inside your wrists.
14. Avoid anything negative like the late TV news.
15. Don't overload yourself. Do what you can and move on.
16. Slowly eat a small chocolate telling yourself you will be fine.

17. Write down your problems. What advice would you give a friend with those same challenges?
18. Ask God for guidance and remind yourself He loves you!
19. You can bounce back from anything by talking with God and a good friend.
20. Write down your problems. Then make 3 columns. Label the first one worse possible, second best possible, the third the most likely outcome. This will help you think things through. My philosophy is to prepare for the worst, then pray and hope for the best. Above all else, try to avoid a pity party.

I honestly feel that tough times occur to teach us lessons, and to be more grateful for all the good things in life. Remember you can laugh or cry and it is better to laugh.

Try to put on your happy face. It will make you and others feel better. Just pull up your panties and deal with it.

33

Fun Being a Good Mistress

Bet that gets your attention! Life is short. I just want to have fun, O.K.? I try really hard to be a good mistress. It isn't easy. I try to stay on my toes. However, those spotted creatures are sometimes smarter than I am. How sad is that?

Years ago I had a Dalmatian I called Atlantis Broadway Buster. Maybe it was his name that caused Buster to be so theatrical. He was a top mischief maker! I always have tried very hard to get our dogs into good loving homes. I would not let people come out to see the puppies until I had spent an hour on the phone talking to them. They didn't get one from me if I didn't think "they could be the leader of the pack." They had to have a settled life, a fenced yard, etc. I also checked my older dog's reaction to them and vice versa. (Now, in addition, my co-owners and I require them to fill out an application with all kinds of references which we check.) We also ask that they take them to obedience school. In spite of my efforts sometimes "things happen." I had gotten Buster back three times! As adorable as he was, he was "a handful." He lost his first home due to a divorce. The wife and teenagers had to move into a smaller house without a fenced yard and, working extra hours, the mother felt she was unable to cope with him. Then I co-owned Buster with a teenager and her mom. However, the daughter got lazy and wasn't caring for him, so back he comes. By this time Buster was about a year old. The next home he lost because he had been kept in a pool enclosure during the day. Apparently Buster went through the screening after a squirrel twice. So back he came again! This time with ringworm.

I had absolutely no problem with Buster. But my Hubby felt that having two bitches (girl dogs) and one male were enough with my frequent trips from Florida to Georgia. Thus, I decided to take Buster to our National Specialty Show in Southern California where I might find him a "show home."

Hubby took Buster and me to the Atlanta airport, arriving early. Buster was excited as he joined the rest of the many travelers. He seemed to say, "Isn't it neat all these people want to see me off." He was wagging his tail and having a great time and getting a lot of attention. We arrived at LAX and what do they do, but put his crate on the baggage carousel. Buster thought he was on a merry-go-round! I wasn't as happy as he. We had our Dalmatian Club of America Show near Disneyland, I believe at a Hilton Hotel. We had an area to one side for the actual show. The other side was directly across a small driveway, where we walked the dogs to go potty.

I noticed how happy Buster became on the elevator. I also noticed him looking at the big mat in the front of the automatic sliding front doors. We were rooming with my friends from Massachusetts, Helene and Pauline, sisters and their Best-in-Show bitch Samantha. In hopes of selling him, I had several people come up to the room to see him. Buster was unusual as he was "very" lightly spotted with a very cute face. It was very distinctive as he had spots around his eyes that looked like miniature footballs. One went up and down, the other sideways.

One morning the sisters had a friend visiting. The three of them were sitting on the balcony. Both dogs were loose walking around in the room. I told the girls I was going to take a shower. When I came out there was Samantha, but no Buster. We looked up and down the hall, No BUSTER. (I do not do well in emergencies.) Helene said she would go down to the front desk to see if anyone saw him. I went to look over the balcony as I thought he might have jumped over and was lying in the parking lot dead. Pauline was trying to calm me down. Just then Helene is pounding on the door. We open the door to a happy Buster and laughing Helene. She said, "You won't believe this. I started to press the button for the elevator when the door opens and out walks Buster. No people were in it." Pauline says, "Wonder how he knew what button to push?" Helene said, "I guess he just watched Emily." We thought that the maid had accidently let him out. It took several years for us to put together most of what happened. Tim Robbins was editor of "The Spotter," our quarterly Dal magazine. On his "from the editor" page was a message saying if we didn't take proper care of our dogs in the hotels we wouldn't be invited back. He went on to say that there was a dog seen running up and down the third and fourth floors. One of the people who had looked at Buster told us that he had seen him loose in the exercise area. He had recognized him, and in an effort to find me, took him to the show area, as well as the front desk. The people at the front desk somehow did not have me registered. At that point the elevator door opens; Buster gets loose and runs in. Before this guy could grab him, the door closes. Buster didn't come back down. The sisters tell me later, "Guess what? We found out that Samantha can open doors. (Round ones)."

I did find a lovely lady with a teenage daughter that fell in love with him. Unfortunately, I never got to see him again as he remained in California. Buster however had a long, good, happy life, even though he never got his championships. Bless his spotted heart!

You really have to have a sense of humor and be willing to train your dog. Even then ours would sometimes think and move faster than we did. Early on, two of our champions got into trouble when they quickly got a mouthful of turkey off the dining room table. I had just picked up a couple of dishes of food and was only a few feet away. They also got into trouble at Christmas as they went "bird hunting." They took a couple of artificial birds off my Christmas tree.

Love also got into big trouble when she got out (in spite of my efforts) and went next door and killed the neighbors "pet" chicken. Before she came home she rolled in their horse manure. That was a smelly, tricky situation! If Dals weren't so cute, sweet, loyal, and so much fun, we would kill them. However, you can see how they aren't for everyone.

Our Alex was a "clown" as well. We had just returned from a show weekend. On Monday I had put him out with our two bitches. Suddenly I heard "a lot" of barking. I called the dogs, the girl's came, no Alex. He was barking. It took me at least five minutes to walk the deck, go down stairs and across the back yard to where he was. I couldn't believe my eyes. There was Alex up a pine tree after a cat! He quickly came down, and I still can't figure out how he was holding on. I had trimmed his nails very short on the previous Friday. Alex also did a number on me the next weekend. He won Best of Breed from the Bred by Class with Mr. Dalmatian, Bill

Fetner, who had founded Coachman Kennels. Alex loved showing! When I took him into the group, I sat him up behind a black standard poodle. He was fine until the judge had us "go around." Alex suddenly almost pulled my arm out of its socket. I think he thought she was a "big cat."

Our son, T.J., a young sweet friend of ours, and Alex all piled into my very small Honda (like a VW). We drove to New York for the big Westminster Show complete with Alex's crate on top. (Alex took up most of the back seat—poor T.J.) We checked into the fancy hotel (I believe a Hilton) only to find out we couldn't get into our room for several hours. First I tried charm—"Do you have a dog?" Yes, he did. "What would you do with him if you couldn't get into your room?" They had a huge lobby. I figured if I was obnoxious enough, they would get me into my room faster. (Sometimes I am not too smart. We could have been thrown out.) I ran Alex around the lobby. One of the "A" list professional dog handlers saw him, liked him and wanted me to sell him to a client of his. However, when I found out he would end up in South America, I just couldn't do it. Then all at once, I see a couple with a cute liver (chocolate color) Dalmatian bitch come through the door. I introduced myself. It turns out that even though their little girl wasn't in season and ready to be bred, Alex thought she was. Man was he interested!!! All of a sudden I had AN IDEA! I asked them when they were to get in their room. Like us they had a long wait. I said, "How would you like to get your room now? One of them said, "How are we going to do that?" I said, "Come with me and go along with whatever I say." (They didn't know me, so they trusted me.) We walked our dogs over to the manager's desk. I said, loud enough for the manager to hear. "I guess, since we can't get into out room we'll have to breed them right here." You should have seen the managers face! All of a sudden I was a hotel manager's worst nightmare! He said very disgustedly, "I'll see what I can do." A few minutes later, still very irritated, he hands the key to T.J. and says, "Get your mother out of here, please." Wasn't Alex smart to have helped us in a difficult situation?

I really, really loved showing Alex. However I never was interested in "specialing" a dog. To special a dog means trying to go for group wins and the ultimate Best in Show. I could have and probably would have kept him; however, he was causing some big problems. Three times he jumped a fence and "jumped" Topper, my other male. They loved everyone and got along fine with any other dogs. However Alex had a real problem with Topper. Alex had also gone through my window screen after a squirrel.

Then the mail man said he was running in the road. I finally sold him as a finished champion for about two hundred dollars. Of course I had a lot more invested in him, but he needed to go to a more controlled situation. Handler Pete Dawkins helped me find a lady who loved to special dogs. Pete and Glenda would keep the dog at their place. They had a lovely set-up. He would be in a large high fenced run, their house, or in a crate when traveling. Alex loved them both. I could see him at shows and he would get to do what he loved most, "showing." Alex was a dog that would wag his tail all the time and pull on the lead to get into the ring. He was born and bred to do that. Within six months he was number six in the U.S. However Pete retired, at that time to go into "judging." Alex was shown by "juniors" (young kids) and still was in the top twenty. Several years later I got him back. He was seven and still looked great. Topper had gone to a show home in California, so I didn't have a dog problem.

I was out in the back yard hosing down my wicker furniture getting ready to re-paint it. Alex was with me. He barks, I look up and he runs and jumps our barn gate. Then he barks again and comes back over. He just wanted me to see he could still do it. He still was a "big handful." I feel that people can and do get obsessed with holding on to dogs. They think no one but them can give a dog as good a home. Can you believe, earlier on I had 33 dogs at one time? I know about obsession. (We had two litters consisting of about twenty-four puppies, some teenagers and a couple of adult dogs.)

I had gotten down to just two or three when Alex came back. Again he was jumping the fence (the only jumper I ever had) and running in the road. Pete found him a retirement home with a teenage boy who would take him and run him every day. My life was easier without him, but I do have a lot of Alex moments to remember. If I see Pete or Glenda, they always mention him. He was loved by a lot of people. He still has the number one spot for being "my most fun dog to show." Sometimes being a good mistress is harder than you expect.

34

Fun with Show Biz

I really, really, really wanted to take tap dance lessons from about age four after I saw Shirley Temple dancing in a movie. However, it was never possible. My folks owned one car, and my mother didn't learn to drive until she was 40. Hard to believe, isn't it?

From the time I was 10, I was active in our local 4-H Club. This national rural organization provided learning experiences with all kinds of projects for kids to complete during summer months. When I competed at the county level in a 4-H public speaking contest, I won first place and seven dollars. At age 14, that was a lot of money ($40-$50 today)! I was so surprised that by talking I made money. I thought I should consider some kind of career in "talking".

In 1952 (I was 17), my parents bought our first black-and-white TV set. I remember a classmate saying, "Your life really changes once you have TV." I had no idea. She told me that people dropped in every evening. Since we lived in the country, that didn't happen to us. Our lives did change, though. I loved *I Love Lucy*, like the rest of America. I knew I could play her part.

One day I discovered Ruth Lyons, a celebrity in Cincinnati who had her own talk show (David Letterman's inspiration). The Women's Clubs from all over Ohio and surrounding states made reservations to go to her show. The studio was set up like a 1950s nightclub, with many small tables on different levels. There was a band, a stage, and a dance floor. This gave visiting "acts" (dancers and singers) a place to perform. Ruth interviewed out-of-town celebrities who were in Cincinnati to promote a record or to star in local theater productions. She roamed around the room having fun as she asked questions of the ladies. I wanted to do what she was doing!

In high school I acted in the junior and senior class plays. I often won awards for presentations or papers I wrote. In Washington Court House, Ohio, I was on the radio several times. I was a disc jockey for our Ohio State University radio station.

In order to graduate as a speech major, I needed to take a foreign language. Most of the girls in my Spanish class at Mary Washington College had taken Spanish in high school. I had taken Latin. A hearing discrimination problem made it very difficult for me.

No doubt, having a room off campus and having to share a double-bed with my roommate wasn't helping. (We barely got along.) Maybe I should have tried French. I definitely should have gone to the Dean of Women and would have if I had been savvier. Fortunately, it was only one semester.

Moving around the country with Hubby, I used my speech classes in many ways. I became president of several groups. When I taught, I always had the students do oral reports. In Atlanta, I appeared on TV with my Dalmatians a few times to promote upcoming dog shows. Fun!

In the '90s a couple of friends encouraged me to do stand-up. In Orlando I competed against young adults. They, of course, had their friends in the audience; I didn't, and still I won second out of eight contestants (the amount of applause determined winners). In Atlanta I took classes in stand-up comedy and found it is NOT easy. A comic has to start and end with a WOW joke. You write your own material and need the jokes to flow well. Graduation included an appearance at The Punchline Comedy Club, in front of about 250 people. It can be overwhelming. It can also give you a real rush if all goes well and they love you. I was fortunate that it went very well.

Did I think about becoming a professional? Yes, I talked to the professionals and asked a lot of questions. (I've worked in market research, so I always check things out.) It takes a while to get to the paid level. There is a lot of travel and not the best accommodations. Most clubs allowed smoking—ugh! I love to travel, but I'm not a good traveler. I decided it wasn't for me. Would I do stand-up again? Maybe.

In 2002 I was an extra in the movie *Sunshine State*. It starred Edie Falco, Angela Bassett, Mary Steenburgen, Gabriel Ferrer, Alan King, and Timothy Hutton. We had to be on set at 7:30 AM, dressed as we would to attend a small-town fair. (I could never be a movie star because of all the "hurry up and wait.") We were given lunch, but not with the stars. In one of "my" scenes I was in front of Brett's Restaurant, selling cookies for a local church, as background for a Mary Steenburgen scene. They did it over four or five times. I found Mary to be very slender and very professional. In another scene, Gabriel Ferrer, Debbie Boone's husband, was walking diagonally across the street in front of us. He looked a lot like his dad, the actor Jose Ferrer (uncle of George Clooney). They wrapped at about six thirty. A very long, interesting day. I loved watching the hunky director and his assistant working their magic! It was fascinating, but they cut the scene I was in. With the $65 I earned, I purchased a silver shell ring in Naples, Italy. I call it my movie star ring. That has a certain "ring" to it, doesn't it?

Remember the movie, *Breakfast at Tiffany's*? If you haven't seen this classic, do. Filmed in New York in 1961, it starred Audrey Hepburn and George Peppard. One of my Ohio State University suite-mates in the late '50s was Beth, who was close to her cousin, George. Whenever George was on TV in *Playhouse 90*, Beth and I watched in our dorm lounge TV room. (No one had TVs in their rooms and few had one at home.) When the *Breakfast at Tiffany's* movie came out several years later, of course I had to see it. George and Beth looked so much alike—similar blue eyes. Those of you who are younger may remember George as the attractive older lead in the TV series, *The A-Team*.

In the mid-'70s George came to Atlanta for the lead in *The Sound of Music*. My friend, Sara, and I went to the theater to see him. I sent a note backstage that I was Beth's college friend. She and I had lost touch. Sara and I tried to see him at the stage door, but missed him.

The next day the phone range, and this deep, sexy voice said, "Is this Emily Hoover?" My heart almost stopped as he said, "This is George Peppard. I am Beth's cousin." (Like I wouldn't remember that.) I told him how much we enjoyed his performance. I also told him Beth and I used to watch him on TV. He was very charming and gracious as we caught up on Joan. He said he would be having Thanksgiving dinner with her. I walked on clouds for a few days. He died young, of lung cancer. Unfortunately,

I understand he was a heavy smoker. (If you smoke, PLEASE STOP. It is much easier today, so says Dr. Oz.)

This reminds me: I need to see if I can locate Beth again. This also reminds me of a very daring thing Beth talked me into. She was from Dayton, Ohio, where I was working. She called and told me we should "crash" an upcoming wedding. I do wild things at times, but I never would have thought of doing that! Actually, Beth was very sweet—not one to do wild things. The wedding was at the Methodist church where she and her family were members. She had read in the paper about a dance studio owner having a huge wedding. She felt we should go to get ideas for my upcoming wedding. She said that since the bride owned a dance studio, everyone would think we had been in one of her classes.

So we dressed up and off we went to the biggest wedding I have gone to, ever. It was unbelievable! The procession included eight flower girls, one maid of honor, and 21 bridesmaids. Of course all of those beautiful young women had handsome escorts. It was like an old 1930s *Ziegfeld Follies* movie. Any moment we expected a big dance production. Think of Buzz Busby's ooh-la-la dance numbers. The female attendants wore long, flowing pastel gowns with a big ruffle that extended across the top and over the arms, and another large ruffle at the hem. Keep in mind, with the bride and groom there were 50 in the wedding party. I wonder if the marriage lasted.

Beth and I guessed that the bride was "older," maybe 28 to 30. We figured she had been a multi-multi-multi bridesmaid. Maybe she was president of her sorority and had lots of girl friends. Or maybe she was poor at making decisions. She probably was used to orchestrating big dance recitals. Talk about show biz.

She must have had a rich daddy or a super-successful business. Most department stores like Macy's were beginning to offer installment plans, especially on appliances and other expensive purchases. Some stores offered a layaway plan. (I had put my wedding dress on layaway over a year before our big day, since Hubby and I paid for our own wedding. This was in the days before MasterCard.) Beth and I were the last to leave, so we pulled it off. We didn't try to crash the reception.

I met show-biz celebrity Brett Butler in the early '90s when I was doing some stand-up. I had seen Brett on late-night TV. She came to do a large show in Atlanta. My friend, Elsie, and I went to see her. After the show Elsie and I got to meet her. Brett is a funny, sexy, pretty, southern gal with a strong personality. Definitely fun, fun, fun! As I gave her a T-shirt, I told her I did some stand-up and also raised and showed Dalmatians. I had done some Dal art on the shirt, which I told her about. She said "Cool." We thought she was really nice.

Funny thing happened! I got a real sweet thank-you note from her. She teased me, though, since I guess somehow that particular T-shirt did not get printed. So the joke was on me. I was in the process of moving and didn't get around to sending her another. I think I have a couple left. Maybe I'll send her one . . . now 15 years later and see what happens. Many of you probably remember Brett from her sitcom, *Grace Under Fire*. She was the attractive, blonde, fast-talking, blue-collar, single mother, factory worker. It is always good to see someone who works hard "make it big time." I always enjoyed her work. Recently I saw and enjoyed her on TV in a movie, *Bruno* (2009), where she plays an old-fashioned, habit-wearing nun who's a spelling teacher. Hey folks, isn't life FUN?

35

Fun Looking Good

When you are young someone may tell you that you are beautiful. They could be lying to get in your panties. If it is an old lady, her sight may be going. Regardless, beauty doesn't last forever unless you have pricey plastic surgery, like Joan Rivers. I think she is not only beautiful, but always looks fabulous. Even though she is short, she looks dramatic. I noticed she always wears a basic black outfit topped by a colorful jacket. I got a red jacket of hers from QVC that I love.

Women often ask me where I buy my clothes. I really believe it is not where you buy them; it is how you put them together. Are the colors good on you? Are the right proportions, right size and type for YOUR body shape? For instance, since I am tall I look better in longer tops or jackets over long pants to hide the sagging stomach. Hubby used to love how I looked in a turtleneck and a long, dressy, straight skirt. Now who knows?

A much younger Dalmatian friend said, "I hope I look as good when I get to be your age." I joked and said, "You don't look that good now." She walked right into that one, didn't she? With a Ph.D. and knowing me for a long time she should have known better. Thank God she has a wonderful sense of fun. Now she needs to get me back.

If you want to improve your image, study fashion books from the library before checking current trends in magazines. The books will tell you how "to deal with" wide shoulders, a big bust, heavy waist, etc. You need to wear what is flattering and age appropriate. Just because short skirts may be "in" they may not be the best length for you. If you are tall you can wear more dramatic clothes. If you are short, you will look better in single-color outfits. If you wear a top and pants the same color, with heels, you will look leaner and taller. It is all about line, proportion, color, and texture. Any fabric that reflects light adds pounds. Getting the length right is so important. Our pants should brush or almost brush the tops of our feet. Capri pants look better than shorts on heavier older women. Notice what other women your size and height look good in. Consider the entire picture: accessories, footwear, and handbag. Don't let a salesperson talk you into anything. Take it home, try it on, and really look at yourself in a long mirror if at all possible. If it doesn't look good front and rear, return it. Most important is do you love it and do you expect others will love it on you? Don't buy something just because it's a good deal.

Get your clothes right, and all you'll need is a good hairstyle and makeup. For a good cut, ask women who have one, where they go. They'll be flattered. The best things you can do for your skin are eat fruits and vegetables and drink eight glasses of water every day. I know at first it will be difficult. I had a problem doing this, before I had kidney failure. As to actual makeup, Maybelline was good enough for glamorous Eva Gabor, a 1950-'60s B-movie star, and I used Maybelline for years. I still use Maybelline Big Lash and their lipstick.

A few years ago I asked my hairdresser if she ever knew of anyone who used mineral makeup. She said *she* did. I joked, "Maybe you should change." At my stage in life, I use a night cream (which I like a lot: M. Asam from Home Shopping Network). Under my makeup I use L'Oreal with sunscreen. Presently I use a cream make-up made by Elizabeth Arden. Younger women can get by with less makeup coverage than some of us.

Facial hair can be controlled by a prescription cream, razor, laser, or a doctor-prescribed pill. Do the laser early because it does not kill gray hair.

You can get a machine that will airbrush makeup on, like movie stars and Kelly Ripa use. I saw it on one of the shopping channels. Question: How can you do it without getting it in your eyes? And won't it clutter up your bathroom?

There is a "mini-lifestyle lift" that lifts anything south of the nose. It is not as invasive as a full facelift and only takes an hour. At 50 my friend, Karen, had a jowl problem and she had the mini-lift. Karen said she could hear the doctor, but did not feel the pain. She went back to work after a few days. She said she would do it again. It cost $2,000, but insurance does not cover this surgery.

I wanted to do it, but Linda, my vet Dal pal talked me out of it. She was concerned about my kidneys. Darn it, I'm the one who told Karen about it. I would look a lot better. Darn!

If you keep healthy, trim, and well groomed, you will have more self confidence and more fun as you look better in your clothes. As you age this is more important.

I frankly have never understood why some older ladies stop wearing make-up or stop coloring their hair. It does take time, but the rest of us that look at you appreciate your efforts. It is a known fact, people respond better to attractive people. The choice is yours.

36

Fun with Dog Show People

Usually show dog people are fun, but very competitive. We may not be super friendly when getting into the zone, before going in the ring, or if your dog beats theirs.

Dog shows are usually safe places for kids.

Before leaving home, I'd say to my dogs, "Do you want to go to a dog show?" They would get so excited because they got lots of attention and ice cream afterwards.

Years ago a pal of my son T.J.'s went with us to the Atlanta show, near our home. While I was chatting with a friend, T.J. took one of our dogs to the van. (The dogs always had fresh water and treats as they happily jumped into their crates.) He returned to tell me we had to stay for Best in Show. He overheard a professional handler talking about a "streaker" hired to appear during Best in Show. (The boys were 12.) I seriously doubted this would happen. However, I love Best in Show. We stayed.

After the judge moved the dogs around the ring, a young gal in a raincoat with a wide-brimmed hat appeared. She quickly removed her coat and ran nude across the ring in green knee socks. She took off her hat and let her long red hair fall and quickly disappeared. Everyone laughed as the judging continued.

Years later at the Kennesaw show, a buddy of mine said I needed to stay for Best in Show. Being a member of the Atlanta and Kennesaw

Clubs, and the Dalmatians Club, I knew a lot of people. After Best in Show we were invited to stay for a wedding. I didn't know the couple, but stayed anyway.

An old, thin, short minister stepped onto the Best in Show platform. My handler buddy said, "Why don't you call for cleanup in the Best in Show ring, Emily?" "Cleanup" means that someone needs to come clean up poo-poo. The slender bride was long-haired, and wore a flowered filmy dress. The groom was older and shorter. Let's just say neither would win a Best in Show.

These two stories are not the norm, but we love to talk about them because they are so unbelievably funny.

At a show in Athens, Georgia, I see a handler friend, Big Guy, who was there and showing our "Top Spot" for his then owners. (Before I got him back for digging up her tulip bulbs). Big Guy asked me, "How I was doing?" I replied I had a large tumor that had to be removed. (Cancer, grade 1.) He loves to tease and so do I, but that day he was very sweet. Years later, he is a judge and writes interesting articles for dog magazines. I always have fun with him and his wife.

I've always envied couples who show dogs together. My Hubby always loved the dogs, but never liked to go to shows. He said it was no fun holding on to a couple of dogs while I "talked pedigrees."

Since Chows usually show before Dals I got to know some of the people. Frequently the Chows I liked, won. For years I saw two couples. One day I noticed they had switched partners and remarried.

One of the Chow people called and asked if I'd judge an all Chow match, since the Chow breeder judge was ill. Matches are casual shows for young dogs and wannabe judges. There were over 30 Chows. The boy I chose went reserve at their national Chow Specialty show and finished his championship that weekend. The bitch I put up was in the ribbons at national and also got points that weekend.

Judging matches is a training experience and considered an honor. The club usually gives the judge a nice gift. I saw, out of the corner of my eye, a 12" x 40" darkly stained piece of wood with a Chow head carving surrounding a clock. The perfect gift for Best of Breed; however it was my gift. For once I was a lady, smiled and said, "Thank you very much." I put it on my memory wall and grew very fond of it.

I must warn you that dog show people can be a bit "earthy." Sometimes, breeders have to help put the penis in the bitch. We scoop lots of poop.

We deliver puppies, which is a yucky, yucky, yucky experience. And if you have never experienced feeling hot poo-poo through ripped puppy papers, you haven't lived. Maybe that is why most of us enjoy gross stories.

Socially, I know a lot of sweet, old-fashioned grandmother types. They don't understand me, but some maybe even like me. At dog shows you will find some older gals as bad as me.

At a show I was chatting with an exhibitor I have known for years. I said, "Your Dalmatian has the most awesome testicles I have seen." My buddy blushed. I said, "I have never seen anything like this. "He had a white spot on each of his black testicles." Had I been judging, your dog would have won everything!"

Then I told my friends they needed to ask to see this dog's testicles. I told his wife what I said to her husband. She laughed. It just proves God isn't done with me. You can laugh with me or at me—as long as you "laugh."

My point is, you can be a grumpy or a positive fun person at any age. The choice is yours every minute of every day; I try to be sweet and nice. With a negative Mother, it was not easy.

Another long time buddy of mine likes to "get me verbally" every time he can. He and his lovely wife and I co-bred a litter of Dals. He phoned me a while back disguising his voice. He asked, "Is this Emily Hoover?" I said, "Yes." He said, "This is the sexiest and best-looking guy in the world." I was thinking, *Who is this NUT?* Finally I said, "I thought that was my Hubby, sitting across the room." When he laughed, I recognized his voice. I said, "You bada**, you." What fun he is.

At our National show his wife and I were chatting. He came up and started teasing me, so I pinched his butt. I said, "I just found out you're a brief type of guy." His wife laughed, "Yes, he is." He blushed and probably for the first time in his life was—speechless. Ho-ho-ha-ha! Gotcha back! He should know not to mess with this old bitch.

Want to go to a dog show? Pull up A.K.C. on the Internet for upcoming shows. You can pull up a judging schedule for the day and breed you want to see. (It is available a week ahead of time.) Go and have a great time! You'll notice that the judge and the exhibitors are dressed up.

While you're at the dog show, notice how some of the people resemble their dogs. Don't pet a dog unless you ask the person handling the dog if you may. Extend your hand, palm up, towards the dog. Just because a dog is at a show doesn't mean he has passed a temperament test. Frankly, in my opinion, a dog should have to pass a temperament test before becoming a champion. I am appalled at seeing and hearing of top winning dogs with serious personality problems.

If you love a breed, are somewhat competitive, like to do things with your pet, like to have fun, and don't mind some travel—showing dogs might be a great hobby for you or your family. (Entries usually cost $25.00-30.00. For more information go to the American Kennel Club.)

As my youngest wrote in an article when he was 10, "Dog shows teach you life isn't always fair."

37

Fun with Dentists

Dentists, I have found, are usually more fun than MDs. Maybe this is because you spend more one-on-one.

Growing up, I had absolutely horrible experiences with our family (sadist) dentist. He NEVER used Novocain. Talk about pain!

At Ohio State my roommate, Mary Lou, was studying to be a dental hygienist. So our friends went to the dental school for dental work. While having my wisdom tooth removed I passed out. An instructor brought me around. They had given me a local anesthetic, but in order to calm me they needed to find a vein. After four or five tries, finally an instructor inserted the IV.

It was NOT fun, as my jaw was too small and the third molars came in under the gums horizontally. The dental surgeon had to go through the gum and cut/saw the tooth in half to extract it. Definitely NOT something I would wish on anyone. (Well, maybe a rapist or a terrorist. Dear God, it is very difficult to "love neighbors" like that.)

Admittedly, I was young and stupid. I had a date on the Saturday evening after the surgery on Friday. What was I thinking? I had a date with a dental student to go see and hear the jazz legend Stan Kenton. I was in bed all day on pain pills. It wasn't easy to go out and have fun. I must have been boring, too, since that was the last date I had with that guy.

Eight months into my marriage I went to the dentist (our neighbor) for a check-up and cleaning. It was a low blow when I found out I had cavities in most of my molars. He knew my fear of dental work and explained every problem in detail. He said that since I was about five months pregnant, the baby may have been drawing calcium from my teeth. However, the main problem was that my childhood dentist had not gotten all the decay out. A good dentist not only removes visible decay, but takes a little extra to make sure he gets it all. (Kind of like cancer surgery.)

Now I have two really good dentists, one in Florida and one in North Carolina. These guys are not only experts, they are fun guys. The Florida dentist is probably a runner and kinda reminds me of TV talk show host Craig Ferguson.

The older a person gets, the more our medical professionals want (or need) to see us in order to keep us healthy. If you don't floss well and brush correctly, you can (and I did) get gum disease. If you have much bleeding when having your teeth cleaned you definitely need to do a better job.

Frankly, I thought Dr. Gingivitis was maybe too proactive . . . until I saw how my gums healed with the right care. (Now I get cleanings about three times a year and have healthy gums.) Dr. Gingivitis, although pleasant, sweet, and caring, smiled but didn't seem to laugh at my lame jokes.

I told Faye, "If he doesn't laugh soon, I am going to have to do something drastic."

"I'll have to think of something. . . . Hey, Faye, I might say, "Doctor, you may need to examine your zipper" She grinned and said, "You wouldn't, would you?" Turns out that I didn't. He said, "You look really good today." I replied, "Pity you don't." And he laughed heartily. He doesn't know how lucky he was, does he?

For years when living in Atlanta, I was the patient of a dentist I'll call Dr. Wellness. He was an older guy, skilled, kind, and sweet. He redid many of my fillings.

Hey guys, now is the time for "the facts of the mouth and teeth." You young people need to realize that, yes, <u>what you do today will affect you the rest of your life</u>. And yes, you'll probably live a long time. My advice is to get a good dentist. Talk to older people and ask where they go. We want skilled and reasonable. Do get your teeth cleaned twice a year. Floss and brush at least twice a day. If you don't, you are headed for dental hell. My friend Randy, who didn't take care of his teeth, started losing them at 20! He didn't eat a balanced diet and loved sweets. Jessica, my dental hygienist, told me to quit crunching on ice if you don't want to break your teeth.

Sometimes, in spite of your best efforts, a healthy diet, and care, you may need fillings due to bad genes. Not fun, but not the end of the world either. Sometimes a filling will crack. It needs to be removed ASAP. Hopefully you can get it refilled. However, sometimes a crown is necessary. Big bucks, but necessary. Why not just have the tooth pulled? (I opted to do this with a rear molar and would do it again, but NOT for other teeth.) If you have any other teeth pulled, this causes your remaining teeth to move. If you don't suck it up and get those necessary fillings or crowns, not only will you have disgusting black teeth that HURT BIG TIME, you are now really ugly. In addition you need to know that the decay in and from your teeth goes into your bloodstream and affects your heart and can cause premature DEATH! Better—preventive care.

Dr. Young, who replaced Dr. Wellness, was in his 30s. He was an adorable blue-eyed, blond hottie. Just the kind of guy you want touching you. OK, it was all professional, darn it. I loved to joke with him. He told me some really silly Louisiana jokes.

In addition to being a "doctor's worst nightmare" I am probably a "dentist's worst nightmare." After the horrible dental experiences of my childhood I AM NOT an easy patient. I try to be pleasant and fun so they'll give me plenty of Novocain.

Dr. Young's office had an open atrium with the center part featuring plants and artwork. Off this area radiated the waiting room and offices. One day after hearing the bad news about some extensive/expensive repairs I needed, I said, "Dr. Young, I feel that after all the years of dental work I have had, I need to plan on doing myself in, in this chair." He was speechless for a second and then he shushed me. He said, "Please don't talk so loud. The other patients may hear you." I said, "I think it could be really interesting as to how you could get a body out of here." He asked me to open my mouth, and started working.

I hate few things, since I try to be positive, but I really, really, really hate being in the dentist's chair. I think about dying right there. The more I think about it, the funnier it gets. Dr. Young, I'm sure, would panic. I think he would be saying, "Oh no, God, not me. Not in my chair. Why oh why, God?" Then he'd place one of those dental bibs over my face. First he'd have checked to see if I was still breathing by positioning the little mirror in my mouth or up to my nose. Then maybe he'd be glad he had already seen most of his patients earlier in the day.

I wondered what he'd do next, if he had patients waiting and needed that equipment. Of course he wouldn't want to call the paramedics during business hours. In the meantime, rigor mortis would set in. If so, would I go out on a stretcher in a sitting position? Wonder how the paramedics get people to the funeral home. Do they have to break leg bones and hip bones to flatten a body's position?

After a few visits I was back to being me, and the world was good again.

In North Carolina I needed a cleaning, so I called Dr. Lang. I spoke to a sweet lady, who made my appointment. When I went in, I discovered that she had misunderstood me. Instead of booking me for a cleaning I had an appointment with the dentist.

To Ms. Front Desk, I said, "I thought I was getting a cleaning."

The dental hygienist was fully booked for the next couple of weeks. The gal I spoke with must have talked with Dr. Lang.

He came out to the waiting room and introduced himself and said, "If you don't mind waiting a few minutes, I can clean your teeth—if that's OK." Dr. Lang and I hit it off. He asked me if I had spoken to a woman with an accent. I said, "Yes, she was a bit hard to understand, but very nice." He grinned and said, "That was my wife. She does my books and sometimes answers the phone, but sometimes she misunderstands people." With his fun nature I could call him Dr. Jolly. He is skilled, honest, and sweet. When I asked him about a pricey procedure, he explained that he uses a dental clinic that is pricey but has top quality. I don't argue, but damn it—to pay big bucks and then have to go through the procedure as well, somehow seems unfair.

Life isn't fair! This old bitch should know that by now. My husband and I have never had dental insurance, so thank God for credit cards and thank God eventually we can pay them off.

The next year, when in North Carolina, I went for a dental cleaning. I noticed a lot of photos of beautiful smiling young people. "What the heck are all these about?" I asked Dr. Lang. He said, "I do Lumineers® veneers." This is what the stars have done to improve the color and shape of their teeth he tells me. Dr. Lang (late 50's) with his pink cheeks, and with extra padding, a white wig and beard, could be a jolly Santa. I said to him,

"You ought to have some old farts hanging up here, like you and me." He grinned—bless his heart! He really is adorable.

One time while I was in his office, I met his cute wife of Asian descent. She had a great smile and personality. She had her teeth bonded by the "big guy." She loves it when I give him a rough time. I had started calling him Dr. Lumm (for Lumineers®) Lang. I just love the way that sounds!

We eat at Yati, his wife's, restaurant, in Franklin whenever we can. (It is small and very good.) As I told Dr. Lumm Lang, we would go more often if we didn't have to shell out so much at our dentist's. Poor man, if I'm not teasing him, Yati is.

It isn't fun to go to the dentist, but these doctors can be fun. Here's hoping you take care of what God gave you. Don't forget to ask what to do if you have a weekend dental crisis. There are no dental emergency clinics that I know of.

It's not like we can take you to an emergency vet clinic, is it?

38

Fun with an Incredible Woman

Through the years I have met a lot of really incredible women. One of them was Rola whom I met when she was 50. She was born in 1906, before automobiles, telephones, TVs, toilets, and before radios were popular. She was born in the New Bremen community (north of Dayton, Ohio) in the horse-and-buggy days. Her grandparents were from Germany.

Rola, who grew up on a farm, was an attractive girl with brown hair, hazel eyes, a winning smile, and a great personality. She was very bright and at sixteen graduated from high school. She went to business school in Dayton and began working at Wright-Patterson Air Force Base.

During this time she became engaged. She learned to play golf and to dance. This was during Prohibition (the 1920s), a time for knee-length flapper dresses and bootleg liquor served in speakeasies. Most young men were saving up to buy a Ford car with a rumble seat. Simpler times, when Americans were merely hoping to get indoor bathrooms and motorcars.

While Rola was engaged, another man insisted on seeing her. She told me they dated "on the sly." Before long, though, the new man, George, told her she had to make a choice. He told her he loved her and wanted to marry her as soon as possible. He won over her family and they were married. The young couple loved his sister Dorothy and her husband Clarence and they had loads of fun together. I never met George, but I met and loved Dot and Clarence who were always telling funny stories.

I heard about the time Clarence came home to find an unexpected baby grand in their living room.

One time they all went to drink and dance at a speakeasy. Rola laughed as they told the story about her dancing on a table top! She tried to help a contortionist who had turned himself into a human pretzel.

George, like most, took up his father's profession. He sold insurance. In those days married women took care of their families and their apartment. If a woman worked, it looked like the man couldn't provide. In the next few years they had two adorable sons.

George got super sunburned on a family vacation. He'd had rheumatic fever as a child and this sunburn affected his heart. He was bedridden. After a while Rola hired daytime help so she could return to work at Wright-Patterson. It was a very difficult time. She told me it was hard to get someone to care for a baby, a toddler, and a sick man and to clean, cook, and do the laundry. This required using a ringer washer and hanging the clothes to dry. Then everything needed ironing. Rola told me she went through a series of housekeepers. When one of them quit, she found all the clothes (unironed) piled in the closet. Finally she had to hire a nurse. One day George asked Rola why she was avoiding him. The nurse had told Rola to leave her husband alone as he needed his rest. He was ill for only nine months. Their sons were under three years old when their dad died.

Thank God Rola had her job. Soon she returned to night school to become a C.P.A. It must have been difficult for her to work all day, leave her children and attend a class several nights a week. Talk about stress! All the while Rola was grieving for the man she loved. The Depression had set in. Rola worked hard to keep her job.

When the war started six years later, Rola was able to get a sweet woman to stay at the house full-time while the lady's husband was overseas fighting. The boys were now in grade school, so life was easier.

A church friend of her sons' told me he remembered his parents talking about Rola. There had been a photo of Rola and an article about her life in the Wright—Patterson Air Force Base newsletter. She had become the highest paid woman there. She saved her money, bought a car, then a small house as she put away some for the boys' college education and a rainy day.

Rola was active in the Lutheran church and making sure the boys attended Sunday school and Boy Scouts. They were good kids, but very adventurous—like walking on top of an old, iron, framed bridge. Rola would hear what the boys were up to from relatives and neighbors. The younger son recounted an adventure of walking their bikes up and essentially "flying" down a very steep hill. They hoped a train wasn't coming. I saw the hill and was appalled anyone would attempt such a feat.

After the boys were in college, Rola remarried, retired, and moved to Florida. She and her husband bought a small six unit motel on a busy street in St. Petersburg. Before long her husband was bedridden with cancer, and a year later he died. Luckily, Rola was able to sell the motel in spite of Rte. 75 taking the business away. She lost money. She moved back to Dayton, was rehired at Wright Patterson and rented a nice two-bedroom apartment near church and friends. This is when I met Rola.

I knew and loved her about 40 years. You see, I married her youngest son. She wasn't just my mother-in-law, but a really good friend. It has been about 15 years since her death and I still miss her. She was one of those people who—well, to know her was to love her. She was a supportive mother-in-law and loved to have fun. I never saw her depressed or upset. She told me she loved me because "I told it like it was." Ho-ho! (Surprise, surprise, surprise.)

My fondest memory is one New Year's evening. My husband, Mom, and I had dressed up and had gone out to dinner. After a long wait, she suggested we take our knives and hit our wine glasses to get some service. My husband was speechless. What could the poor guy do when his mother and his wife were embarrassing him? Maybe one too many glasses of wine, you think? Maybe that's how she came to dance on the table.

Thank you, God, for allowing her to be an inspiration and a part of my life. I KNOW she would love my book as much as I know my own mother probably would NOT.

39

Fun with the Magic Jacket

My doctor, who I'll be calling Dr. Best, had ordered blood tests. Since Hubby and I have moved many times and have had a lot of different doctors, we feel he is "as good as it gets." However, Dr. Best does like to run a lot of tests. (Maybe I should call him Dr. Covering His Assets.) Actually, I once asked him if he was covering his ass or his assets. He grinned and said, "I just want to take good care of my patients." What do you say to that? I hate it when guys leave me speechless, don't you? Though I do have to tell you I love "bright guys" and I am NOT often speechless.

Frequently I stay up late, writing and/or watching TV. I get up about nine. The day I arrived at the hospital, I finally arrived around ten thirty, of course without breakfast. My favorite blood-letter told me Dr. Best wanted a urine sample as well as my blood. I asked her if she could draw the blood first and she replied, "Yes." Since I have veins that jump around, I get *very* uptight. We started talking about my book, and I forgot about the urine sample.

Afterwards I stopped for a light breakfast, then exercise at Curves, before running a couple of errands. It was a beautiful day, and since we'd had a very cold winter in Florida, this day was to be cherished. I used my cell phone to ask Hubby if he wanted to meet at the Eat-n-Drink Grill for lunch. This restaurant has an open porch and a view of the water. We had a delightful lunch. Hubby told me that the hospital had called and wanted me back for the urine sample. I said, "I can't believe they called so soon. Dr. Best must be waving his whip." After lunch I told Hubby I'd run by the hospital, pee in the cup, and then finish my errands.

Our small hospital has a lot of friendly retired people who volunteer. I walked up to a tiny table where an older guy was seated. Standing next to him was a tall man. The guy at the table said, "You're the woman I've been trying to track down. You're Emily Hoover, right?" "Yes," I replied, and before I could add anything else, one of them said to this friend, "Doesn't she look like a model?"

Keep in mind that this was the day before my 75th birthday and I was 20 pounds overweight, so hearing this STUNNED me.

Before I could speak again, the other man said, "Look how her top matches her lipstick." "Wow," I replied, "my husband of over 50 years never notices stuff like that!"

After hearing these compliments, I was thinking these guys either had a comedy routine or were gay.

The taller one said, "But I've always liked tall girls." The man at the desk then asked the tall man, "What would your wife think of that remark?" He said, "Probably not much. Maybe I ought to go home."

I had on a Diane Gilman jacket that I had purchased a year before from HSN (Home Shopping Network). It is dark denim with gold piping around the cuffs and a stand-up collar. It has gold-trimmed epaulets with gold buttons. With this, I was wearing dark denim boot-cut trousers (dressier than regular denims), a red turtleneck sweater, red glasses, gold hoop earrings, and red loafers, and carrying a large yellow bag my friend Sandy had given me. Remember, I may be 20 pounds overweight, but I am "well groomed." I have to say that even though these guys were "crazy," they made my day! I really felt like they had their act down pat.

Before I could sit down, a beautiful "50s" gal walked up to the "table guy." After being introduced to her, I said, "Oh, are you his wife?" (When will I ever learn to keep my mouth shut?) "No," the man at the table replied (much too fast). "Oh, your girlfriend?" I asked. "No," he said, laughing. "She is my lady friend." I spotted a magazine wall rack with a magazine that had a black cover with big white letters on it that read: SIN NO MORE. Being the bad girl that I am, I pointed to the magazine and said to the couple, "Maybe you two should read that magazine." Fortunately, they thought this was funny.

A month later (wearing the same outfit), I was back at the same table for another test, and to my surprise I saw the same volunteer. He greeted me, picked up the phone, and called his friend to let him know that I was back. While I was waiting, his lady friend also popped in. Either they are "very close" or she is keeping tabs on her guy. He is a lot of fun and so is she.

After getting my blood drawn, I went to the cafeteria for a snack. That day I arrived around ten forty, but due to computer problems at check-in, it was now eleven forty. I planned to meet some of my girl friends across town for lunch around twelve thirty. I was late taking my meds and had to take them with food, so I grabbed some cottage cheese. There were no empty tables.

I approached a table and asked the volunteers if I could sit with them. These people were really fun. We talked about some of the people we all knew. They encouraged me to volunteer so I could hang out with them. I explained to them that I didn't have much time because I was busy writing a book. They asked what it was about, and I told them. They said that it should be fun. I asked them, "Do any of you have any good sex stories for my chapter, 'Fun with Sex'?" They all laughed, and as I was getting ready to leave, one guy did provide a joke for that chapter. They told me they thought I was fun and that I should come back and have lunch with them. Maybe they were being nice because I was wearing the magic jacket. How sweet.

I dashed across town, arriving only a few minutes late. A young man opened the door and welcomed me to the restaurant. He asked me how I was doing and of course I gave him my usual "Fine for an old bitch" response. He laughed. My friends Betty, Judy, Loretta, Karen, and Sandy were already sitting near the front door. We ordered, and while waiting for the food one of the gals asked if I was wearing the magic jacket they had heard about. I said yes and told them about my fun time at the hospital. Before our food arrived, the host approached the table and said I reminded him of his favorite aunt. He went on to say I looked like a model. (Can you believe?)

As they were all laughing, Judy said, "She got that jacket from the Michael Jackson estate sale." That really got me. I have never been a big fan of his. Judy then added, "However, I want that jacket when you get tired of it." I said, "You'll have to lose some weight first." Judy was recovering from cancer surgery and was on steroids and had gained some weight. All of us have weight issues. Fortunately, Judy giggled with us.

Hey people, don't mess with me . . . verbally, I can be DANGEROUS!

So, was it the magic jacket I had on? Or could it be the neat yellow bag Sandy gave me? Who knows? I did wear the same denim outfit to the recent Dalmatian Club of America Welcome Party. Guess what? The magic jacket had a lot of fun!

Speaking of jackets, my friend Judy just called and told me to turn on the TV. Comedian Sarah Silverman was on. Judy and I watched together as we chatted. Sarah was promoting her new book, *The Bedwetter*. And I thought *I* had trouble growing up! The front cover photo pictures Sarah in a military Navy jacket, similar to my magic jacket.

I said, "That jacket might be nicer than mine."

Judy, just home from the hospital, said, "I'm sure it's a much smaller size too!"

She "got me," and we cracked up laughing.

I love how that gal can get me—even in her weakened condition.

I think the Diane Gilman jacket I own has had more fun than Sarah's jacket. What do you think?

40

Fun with Dr. 4 Eyes

I met Dr. 4 Eyes eight to ten years ago. At the time I went a distance to see him at Mayo. He was their glaucoma expert. Yes, I have glaucoma, as do my father and son. It is genetic. The first visit, I was nice, if you can believe it. The second visit, I must tell you about. As you may know by now, sometimes I think out loud.

When Dr. 4 Eyes was putting drops in my eyes I said, "My gosh, you have ice-cube glasses. Isn't there someone younger and cuter here that I could see?"

He grinned and we become instant buddies when he said, "Younger, maybe."

He is an attractive, small-framed guy that I guessed may have come from India. Turns out his parents did, but he was born in Pennsylvania. I quickly got to know him since I needed my eye pressure checked every four months.

Sometime later, he and his wife had a baby boy. He showed me photos. I said, "He's cute."

He later said, "You aren't into babies much, are you?" I replied, "No, I like kids when they can go to the bathroom on their own and can carry on a conversation." All the same, I did love seeing pictures of his child as he was growing.

Whenever the doctor would see me, his cute face would light up. One time I said to him, "How's that ugly little kid of yours doing?" He laughed, and then he told me he was in kindergarten at a Montessori school. I said my great-niece was attending one and that she was learning ballet and Spanish. He said, "She is taking Spanish?" I said, "Yes, she is very bright. Her father is a doctor and her mom has a Ph.D." He had to be thinking, hey, my wife's a lawyer and I'm a doctor. Then he said, "Well, girls start out smarter than boys." When I patted him on the shoulder and said, "Yes, and we stay that way," he laughed. I hadn't seen him for a while because I was in North Carolina. He now had his own practice. Watching him walk towards me and my husband, I guessed to myself that Dr. 4 Eyes had gained twenty pounds. I'd been watching Dr. Oz, and so I was concerned. I said to the doctor, "Are my eyes getting really bad or have you gained weight?" He said, as he grinned, "I look heavier because you have lost weight." He told me he put on twenty pounds in the last six months from the stress of starting a new practice. I asked him where he went to school, and he said he went to Indiana University.

I said to Hubby, "Too bad he didn't go to Ohio State like we did. I know he would have had to take Business 101." Bless him, the doctor just laughed. I asked him to write something down. He said OK. I said, "On www.doctoroz.com, he has some real good tips on weight reduction."

The doctor laughed and wrote it down. I told him my general practitioner wanted me twenty pounds lighter. Dr. 4 Eyes said he was going to start training for a race in May. He also challenged me to lose weight. That should teach me to keep my mouth shut (but I probably won't). He said, "I want to see you in six months." His appointment gal wanted to know what date and I said, "Let's wait. I'm going to be seventy-five soon, so I could die and then I wouldn't have to come back."

He said, "They'll call and remind you." "If you don't reach me," I said, "guess you can figure I'm a goner." I'll make appointments a few weeks or even a month ahead, but not three or four months.

Since I was his last patient that day, I told him I had my dog with me and asked if he wanted to see her. He said, "Sure."

As we walked out, I asked him how his practice was going. He said he was getting a lot of new patients, some even coming from Georgia. I told him I wouldn't drive that far to see him. He laughed again. He gave me a hug as Hubby and I prepared to leave. He is a fun guy and an excellent doctor. Think I'll start calling him Dr. Chuckles since he laughs a lot.

41

Fun at D.C.A. 2010

As always, I plan on fun. The D.C.A. (Dalmatian Club of America) holds an annual large show, this time with 204 Dalmatian entries. We have agility, rally, and obedience classes as well as the conformation show classes. This year it was held in Lawrence, Kansas. I have attended most of the D.C.A. Specialty Shows since 1970. I don't want to miss seeing people and their dogs. I missed a few in the '80s and '90s due to finances and health problems. Now I try to go every year. Hey, I want to have fun as long as I can, baby.

On Saturday I flew from Florida to Atlanta. (If you are going to heaven or hell or almost anywhere else, you HAVE to go through Atlanta.) I remember when it was a rather sweet airport. Now it is huge! Lots of walking, lots of going up and down escalators and getting on and off their famous trams.

I barely made it to the connecting flight—no time for lunch. On Delta they sell snacks, but not much in the way of healthy foods. Are you the kind of person who, if provided a large bag of M&M's will eat every one especially if you haven't had lunch? Well, I am. That and a diet Coke.

A little after one o'clock we arrived in Kansas City. I had arranged to hop a shuttle at three thirty. I headed to the bar for a salad and burger, and a glass of wine. I had a lot of fun chatting with the gal bartender and an

Army medic. I called the shuttle people at three thirty-five, after waiting for them about thirty minutes. Turned out they had showed up at three. They had another shuttle coming at five. That would be another three hours so I rented a car and drove the 65 miles to Lawrence. I could have saved <u>a lot</u> of money by calling the shuttle people the moment I arrived.

A cocktail party with a Western *Gunsmoke* theme would be starting soon. I showed up in denim trousers, a red top, and my "magic" jacket. Of course I was expecting fun! Terri and I had a blast while her husband watched college basketball finals in their room. We both mingled, sometimes together, sometimes not.

Terri is older than the early forties that she looks. She is the kind of gal that guys notice. I never have been. I'm sure Terri is used to lots of flattering comments. She had fun talking to one of the guys that I love to give a rough time to. I think he just loves being around women. His wife is a sweet, lovely woman, and like the rest of us, gets a kick out of him.

He asked Terri what she was showing. She told him she was showing male in the 15-to 18-month-old class.

He said, "I have one in that class, too." He went on to tell her that his dog was very ring experienced and had almost all his championship points. She said, "Mine is just starting to be shown." He then told her his dog moves very well. She replied, "My dog moves well."

He then admitted to her that while his dog was really nice, maybe his front could be better. She said, "My dog has a lovely front."

He told her that his dog had a nice spotting. Terri told him her dog's spotting wasn't bad.

He said, "This show should be interesting," as they grinned at one another.

While Terri was having verbal fun, I was having fun getting photographed with as many guy friends as possible. The plan was to do a collage of lots of "magic" jacket photos as I attended the cocktail party. Terri and I sure had fun.

The next day was our Futurity Show. This involves a breeder-judge who has been chosen by the participating breeders. To be in this show you must nominate your litter before they are born. (You pay a fee every time any of the puppies are nominated.) You evaluate them at birth and again several times as they grow. The "pot" of money is divided among the winners. The money is not that much, but we all like the prestige of winning these special classes.

The class Terri was showing in was very small. The other dogs were shown by their breeders, who had been around more than a few years. The guys Terri was showing against had lots of experience and the judge knew them, so they had the advantage. Terri had bought her dog from my vet co-owner, Linda, and me. A small but tough class. Was I ever proud of Terri and "I Con"! Terri is a master at grooming and keeping a dog at the correct weight and condition.

The night before, I had told her, "Terri, you are here to have fun, meet people, and see their dogs. Don't expect to win. Relax and have fun."

It can be stressful, so I also told her, "No dog is perfect, not even yours."

She was really "high" on him. I'm realistic and think he is lovely, but not perfect. But hey, what do I know? I don't want Terri to get a "big head." There is nothing more obnoxious than someone who has had Dals a few years and thinks they know everything. Even though some of my competitors think I am knowledgeable—after 46 years—I am still learning. Linda and I do a lot of research before we breed anything. We want to avoid genetic problems that have surfaced in the last few years.

Terri's dog came in first in the class. As handler, Terri looked terrific: about a size six, hair with blonde highlights, big blue eyes. She wore lovely cream-colored pants and a cream mock turtleneck with a classy, red double-breasted jacket. Her black patent leather loafers with rubber soles completed her knockout look. Hey, Terri striding alongside a white dog with inky black spots made for a "dynamite package." She went back in the ring to try for the Best Senior, and they received a loud round of applause. The judge, however, gave it to a lovely bitch. Terri had hoped to take it all. I had no problem with what the judge did, though. I was happy Icon won his class. I told Terri her dog only won because she got her toe caught on the mat and fell. Like I said, I don't want her to get too big for her britches.

The D.C.A. had something going on most all day. There is usually time in the afternoon for drinks and fun. One evening we attended an educational program, another night, a meeting. We also had two dress-up evenings. One of them involved a cocktail party with a jazz band. All was fun.

"The Top Twenty Event" is always interesting because a real runway is set up, like that for super models. The dogs ranked in the top twenty are presented by number. Three judges and the handlers are dressed in evening attire. Each of the judges has a scorecard. One at a time, each dog is gaited along the runway by his handler, to his or her own chosen music CD. The judges evaluate the dogs.

After Best of Breed has been determined late that afternoon we have our banquet, usually there are two different winners—even though dogs compete with all the other champions entered, as well as winners dog (male) and winners bitch (female) (top non-champions). In 2010, for example, there were over fifty champions. So to win Best of Breed or Top Twenty is a SUPER honor.

The D.C.A. banquet was a more relaxed event. Terri and her husband decided not to attend since they'd be checking out at 4:30 a.m. So off I went by myself. I reconnected with a gal I had met at my first Atlanta show, where I showed our first bitch. I was cracking her and others up by saying I was 75 and I reminded her I met her over forty years ago, and that she had been my mentor ever since. She later asked me, "How old are you, really?" I told her 75. She said, "You sure don't look it." She even bought me lunch. How sweet. I still owe her, as I bet she forgot about the drink I wanted to buy her. She may be younger than I. Who knows?

I entered the banquet room and spotted (a good word for Dal people) my adorable friend Julia. She's a smart, fun gal. I sat with her on one side and my new friends, Colin and Colin. A new California friend had introduced red-headed Colin to me earlier. She told me he could help me promote my book since he writes blogs and creates websites. I asked him to sit next to me so we could get to know one another. Some other delightful people joined us at our table. Then some people persuaded us to buy tickets for a chance of being on the cover of one of the four *Spotter* magazines that D.C.A. issues annually. This $15 also would give us a chance as an alternate for the cover. And there's more: Chances for published interview!

Wow, I am now an alternate for a cover. If I don't get the cover deal, I'll be given an inside black-and-white ad. Some people buy several chances. That was lucky for me. I've always wanted a cover. We'll see what develops.

Next, D.C.A. "biggies" were selling chances on a really awesome quilt. The night before two quilts went for big bucks in a bidding war. I liked this one much better. All the squares pictured the head of a Dal, which had been appliquéd on and were three-dimensional in some way: a bandanna on one, jewelry on another, etc. And it was beautifully machine quilted. So here they came, hitting me up for more money. I wanted to spend

$5-$10, tops. No way: D.C.A. wanted $20 for 20 tickets. Again, some of the more moneyed people spent a fortune. I felt I had to buy some, so I took twenty tickets. I told several people that if I won, I had no place for it, that it needed to be displayed on a large wall. Guess what? I won it. Wow, wow and double-wow! What a specialty show—our dog won his class, I was having fun, and I won an ad or perhaps a cover . . . and then I won the "big enchilada, the awesome quilt."

What to do? I don't have a place for this. I paint and have always loved wall hangings, so all my walls are taken. At some point in the aging and downsizing process you usually get realistic. So, I started a bidding war at our table for my quilt. One of our D.C.A. cuties offered me $1,000 plus an interview she had won. However, my Irish friend offered doing a blog plus a website and promotion of my book, plus money. I took his offer.

A few of us hung out at the bar. After a while, I left to go to my room since I had a long travel day ahead. On the way to my room, I had checked my secret pocket for my room key. Some gals call it a bra, OK? No key, so I stopped by the desk. A nice-looking, tall, young guy (6'4" I'm guessing, probably thirty or so) was waiting for his free breakfast tickets.

He said to me, "How are you tonight?" I responded with my usual: "Fine, for an old bitch."

He said, "You aren't an old bitch, you're a hot bitch." Honest to God. Would I lie?

Pointing to his beer, I said, "You've had too many of those." He said it was his first, to which I replied, "Yeah, sure." Then I went on to say, "I have 51-and 48-year-old sons, plus a 27-year-old grandson and I am 75." He said, "You don't look it." Fortunately, at that point the guy at the desk gave him his tickets and he left.

The front-desk guy, <u>my only witness</u>, could see how uncomfortable I was becoming. He said, "I was trying to get the breakfast tickets done as soon as possible."

Some of my gal pals would have <u>loved</u> it! Hey, he was a rather cute, tall guy and wasn't mumbling. Had I been younger I would have still walked away. Too bad I am loyal and maybe a nice person (sometimes). Don't you dare count on it, however.

42

Fun Fun and More Fun with Doctors

Dr. Up Yours is my gastro man. You'd probably call him a gastroenterologist. I saw him shortly after one of my bridge buddies said: "If he were single, I could really go for him." When I first saw him—before he closed the door—I said, "A friend of mine has a crush on you. I can't see it; I can't see it at all." Needless to say he was surprised. He quickly replied, "Don't tell me who it is." I said, "Are you kidding? She would beat me up."

A week later I went to the hospital for the "up your butt procedure." They had given me some medication, yet I was still "with it" (as much as I ever am). Dr. Up asked me, "How are you doing?" I said, "Well, keep in mind I haven't had my natural hormones or any real food for two days, and I had a shitty night." He laughed. (Note to you young people: They want to clean you out before a colonoscopy, so they prescribe liquids that make you go and go and go and go.)

After discussing the upcoming procedure, I said, "Your wife is a beautiful lady." He said, "She is very bright too!" I asked him, "If she is so bright, when you asked her to marry you, how did you get her to say yes"? He just grinned and shook his head.

I LOVE, LOVE, LOVE to make bright men speechless.

Dr. Up went across the room to talk to another patient. The anesthesiologist came over, and a nurse said to him, "Your hair is really getting long." He said, "Yeah, I know. I can't understand why six or seven girls aren't lining up to run their hands through it." I quickly said, "Maybe it's the face that goes with it." Yeah, he blushed. Dr. Up Yours laughed and said, "Good! You 'got him'!" Dr. Drug just grinned.

I guess I'm lucky he didn't overdo those "big drugs" on me.

During my follow-up visit with Dr. Up he told me he had removed a couple of growths (painless). They were noncancerous, thank you God! Dr. Up did say he wanted me to be tested again in seven years. This procedure is NOT fun, but after 50 years of age everyone NEEDS to be checked out to stay healthy. Colon cancer is preventable by eating plenty of fruits and vegetables and getting regular check-ups. Keep your weight under control and exercise.

I don't see Dr. Up often, but he always grins as he asks me, "Are you going to give me a rough time today?" I reply, "I certainly hope so!"

My Atlanta gastro guy, Dr. Butt, gave me only enough "gas" to make it comfortable. He said, "You can watch me take the probe through your intestines." Oh, goody, goody, goody, I'm thinking, and said, "Yeah, sure." Actually it *was* interesting, and I talked to his nurse during the procedure. Dr. Butt said, "You girls are going to have to stop talking. I need to concentrate." I was thinking, if you were a woman doctor, you could do two things at once.

Another time, I was sent to Dr. Butt for abdominal pain. He spent almost an hour asking me questions. One question I found interesting was, "Do you ever find you don't have an appetite?" I had to laugh. "Are you kidding? How can you look at me and ask me that?" (At the time I was about 30 pounds overweight.) He grinned. I asked him if he ever saw any "internal" patients. He said, "A few." My Hubby and I went to him until we moved. I find the gastro doctors take a lot more time with you. (Turned out I had to have my gall bladder out—not uncommon for overweight people. Cancer, heart problems, and diabetes, are all related to weight.) Do your best to get and keep extra pounds off, as I am trying to do.

My friend Elsie, who used to work for a proctologist, decided she wanted to get a job closer to home. My dentist needed a receptionist, so Elsie was asking me about him. I said he was a nice guy. I went on to say that if she went to work for a dentist, she would move up in the world.

Another doctor I had an interesting time with was a "heart doctor." I met him at the Cincinnati airport when I asked him for directions. He said, "You can ride over to our gate with me if you like." I just knew he was anxious to get rid of "the talker." And guess what, I just KNEW we'd be sitting next to each other. I just KNEW! Guess what? I was right. The handsome, very slender doctor told me he had recently lost a lot of weight. His mild heart attack had been a "real wake-up call." (Hopefully, you and I won't have to go through that.)

He seemed to enjoy my funny doctor stories. I told him I thought it was too bad most guys are part of the "handicapped species." He asked why. (No matter how bright the guys, they fall into my traps and don't even know it.) I told him that most guys think with what is between their legs, NOT like most women, who think with what is between their ears. Know what? He agreed with me, adding that a lot of bright doctors he knew well messed up their lives BIG TIME. He told me, "I love and respect my wife. She is the mother of my children. I would NEVER divorce her."

At some point I patted him on the shoulder and guess what I discovered? Thin shoulder pads! Honest to God! Was I ever shocked. It's a good thing he wasn't watching my face.

Hubby, usually sensible, did a really dumb thing. He intentionally got up on a tall ladder when I wasn't home. He fell on his back on the tile floor as he sliced tendons in his hand grabbing on to the metal. He cleans up the blood and drives to Curves when he couldn't reach me by cell phone. As I drive him to the hospital I notice blood all over his clothes-ugh-ugh-ugh! A nurse friend told me to soak them overnight in cold water and dry bleach. (After rinsing and regular washing the stains came out. Thank God.) The nurse tells us we are lucky in that Dr. Hand Man is on the island and can do the surgery. He stops to check Hubby several times and tells us he is sorry that due to a backlog it will be about eight before he can do the surgery. We are finally able to leave the hospital around midnight.

A week later we are at Dr. Hand Man's office. I asked him since he is a plastic surgeon why he didn't work on Hubby's face while he was under. He laughed. We discussed my wanting a mini-lift as I pull my turkey neck up and ask him if I wouldn't look better. I tell him I am chicken since I have had kidney failure. Then I ask him if he had thought about having work done himself. He grins and tells me his wife wants him to get his eyes done. I say, "I was thinking more of your jowls." He laughs.

Aren't doctors great? Thank you God.

43

Fun at Funerals

Death can be alarming, fearful, and surprising, yet matters surrounding funerals can be really funny. Have you ever heard of anyone who died "before their time?" Maybe I'm wrong, but I think God plans "our time."

I was 13 when my father's dad died. He was about 64, a tall, big man, a hard worker, a Quaker and a Mason. He never hugged us. My younger sister was afraid of him because he could be gruff. I remember once he was sitting in a rocking chair, fell asleep and was snoring loudly. All of a sudden he woke up and said, "Who is snoring?" I laughed and said, "You, Grandpa." He didn't answer me.

My younger brother, sister, and I were taken to the viewing, but not the funeral.

When my dad was looking over the bills, he started laughing. He told us the funeral home charged him for Grandpa's socks and slippers. They had talked very practical Grandma into buying them. Daddy said, "Where was he going to walk?" Then he added, "Who would see his feet, anyway?" I guess I get some of my sense of humor from Daddy. He seemed to find humor in ridiculous things.

Sometimes the obituaries can be funny. I remember reading a long one in our small North Carolina paper. It listed all the names of the man's family plus the names of those who would miss him. Not unusual, until they started naming his pets. For instance, his dog, cat, hen, and pig—each by name! It cracked Hubby and me up!

A new friend was telling me about an unusual couple in their small town. She said they ALWAYS went to everyone's funeral. What my friend and I found a bit "out there" is that the woman always crammed food into her handbag. An obsession? My friend said she knew that it was not money or a weight problem. I said, "Maybe she likes homemade goodies, but doesn't like to bake or cook." Hey, lady, maybe you ought to leave some for the family.

Recently my Hubby and I lost one of our close buddies, Les. He was 84. He and his wife Viv hiked with my Hubby. The four of us often played bridge together at the senior center. One day after bridge, we went to their house for wine and cheese before going out to eat. Les drove like a race car driver in the hilly college town. Viv and I sat in the backseat and held on to the straps as we wove in and out of traffic. Though it is not always possible to be good friends all four ways, we were, and had taken two fun cruises together.

The next afternoon I ran errands. When I arrived home about three, my Hubby said, "Les died at one." What a shock. I couldn't get Viv on the phone. I made a casserole and we took it to Viv. She was home alone. We shed a few tears.

Soon, Viv's tennis buddies arrived. One of their husbands was a retired attorney. He wanted to know if Les was at the local funeral home. I told him I had spoken to a person at the hospital who said the body had been sent to the crematory in Ashville. Viv said, "No, he was to go to one of the local funeral homes." The body had been missing about four hours before the lawyer found it. In her state of shock, Viv had signed papers she didn't fully understand, and the body went where it shouldn't have. After they found Les's body I said quietly to Viv, "Someday, Viv, this is going to be very funny." Viv gave me a little grin and said, "It's funny now." Love that lady!

Years ago when I worked in Clearwater, Florida, I had a decorating client who had parents that were both 94. Her father had an aneurism, but otherwise they were both in good health. They took short walks every day and enjoyed going out to lunch. Their college roommates had married each other and lived in Sarasota. I never heard of that, have you? Think of it: All of them knowing each other over 75 years. This took place in the 1970s. (These people went to college around 1900, when it was very unusual for women to attend college.) The daughter took her parents to see their friends. Soon afterwards her mom never woke up from her nap.

My friend was en route to the Tampa airport with her dad, to pick up her brother. All of sudden her dad slumped over. Having been a nurse, she knew he had died, but couldn't stop in the middle of the causeway. As soon as she reached Tampa, she pulled over at a rather grand-looking hotel. The manager called an ambulance to take her and her dad's body to the hospital while the manager met her brother's plane. My friend didn't realize what a bad reputation the hotel had (rumors of hookers and crime connections), but thankfully she had a good experience.

I remember many discussions about funerals when my grandmother and others talked about the dead, particularly after Aunt Emily died. The relatives asked each other, "How do you think she looks?" Just how do you expect them to look? Hey, they are dead! They aren't in *Project Runway*. Sometimes you hear "She looks so natural." Aunt Emily, however, didn't look right. Her clothes looked good, but something wasn't right. I realized that they had put really dark makeup on her. Rather weird as her complexion was very fair. I was asking myself why they did this. I later found out that if you die lying on your side, the blood settles there and you get huge black-and-blue areas. If you are planning on an open casket, you might want to sleep on your back.

Me? I am going straight to the crematory. (Doesn't that sound like where you would find ice cream? Yes, I know you go to creamery to get ice cream.) I want to avoid an open casket because I don't want my family to spend money on a casket, etc. I also don't want anyone checking me out. And good heavens, I don't want any of my *never-to-be* "boy toys" to see me like that.

To the "She looks so peaceful" comment, well, why wouldn't she? After all, she doesn't have to deal with you or me or anyone else again. Next time you hear "He looks so natural," you might think, *What do you expect?* In the few days after a person dies, that they have had plastic surgery? Hey, not a bad idea. Think about it . . . no pain! You would go out looking damn good. Think of what people would say: "How did they do that? She looks ten years younger."

I have never seen a fashion article on what a person should wear in a casket, have you? Where are the fashion police when we need them most? Shouldn't a person wear their best casual outfit? Wouldn't it be more appropriate than a beautiful dress? Have you seen people in caskets with their glasses on? Doesn't it look strange with their eyes shut? Maybe they could just be napping and wake up any moment and want to read.

I don't know about you, but I don't attend funeral or memorial services unless I am related or a very good friend. Actually, I'll embarrass you because I could easily be a professional mourner. I could cry at a really bad guy's funeral; I would be feeling sorry for his mama.

I went to a favorite neighbor's funeral when I was four. I recall seeing her in the casket, and everyone looking sad. My mother probably was the saddest as she had lost her occasional babysitter. It wasn't a bad experience. Frankly, I think that seeing all the sad people and having death explained is a good thing. A friend of mine, James F. Weinsier, has written a children's book titled *Where Do We Go?* It's a well-written, award-winning book with attractive artwork that has been a comfort to some kids I know.

I once heard of a mother-in-law and daughter-in-law fighting over the son/husband's ashes. They finally divided them. How, I never heard. No one could make this stuff up—it happened!

Hubby and I had an interesting time writing our will. The lawyer had written that my ashes would be scattered according to the decision of my family. "No, no," I told him, "I want my ashes on the shoreline a few blocks from our home." The lawyer said, "OK, I'll change it." Most people just go along, I suppose.

Hubby and I had a discussion about death. I said, "When I know I'm dying, I want to eat all those goodies I try not to eat now," I said to Hubby. "Like what?" he asked. "Like chocolate brownies with lots of walnuts and plenty of chocolate icing, topped with more walnuts—you know, like I make." "What else?" "Well, German chocolate cake with plenty of icing and pecans, with vanilla ice cream. And pecan pie and vanilla ice cream also peppermint, praline, and pistachio ice cream and lots of cookies."

Where do you think the name "cookie monster" came from, anyway? Then I thought about Becky's super-duper beautiful carrot cake. Hubby said, "We would have to get an extra-big casket." I said, "No, since I am going to be cremated." He said, "They would have to have a big furnace." I said, "Go for it—I am." No, I didn't actually say that. I said, "They could cut me up, what will I care." Sometimes funny things surround death, but I never said it wasn't gross, OK?

My Dal pal, Lucy, called and asked what I was doing. I told her I was finishing the "Fun at Funerals" chapter. She said to tell them about Larry's. (Her husband) Larry was ill for some time before he died. Lucy asked him what kind of service he wanted. "Something simple," Larry answered. He wasn't a churchgoer, but did have a guy friend who was a minister. Larry said maybe he could say a graveside prayer. "That's all you want?" Lucy asked. Larry responded, "Well, maybe you can have the Excelsior's Marching Band." This is a blues band that is big time at Mardi Gras in Mobile, Alabama.

Lucy arranged for the band. Before long, friends reminded her of someone who owned an antique horse-drawn hearse. She and her only daughter had a discussion on what horse could handle the loud music. Finally they found a calm old mule. The plan was for the family to meet at the funeral home. There was no viewing. One of the relatives wanted to see the body. Lucy refused because Larry requested a closed casket. These people decided to go gambling instead of going to the gravesite. Now funny to Lucy.

Lucy's vet offered his horse for "the horseless rider," like Jackie had for President Kennedy's funeral. No doubt this inspired Lucy. Lucy asked the funeral director if they shouldn't be going to meet everyone. He said that Lizzie was late and wasn't cooperating. Lucy's daughter, Elizabeth, thought he meant her. She said, "I'm here and I'm cooperating." That's when they found out the mule's name was Lizzie.

(Reminds me of Oscar Wilde's play, *The Importance of Being Earnest*. A name is important, and the same name can be confusing, can't it?)

The hearse leads the procession, followed by the horse without the rider. The vet carried a tranquilizer in case his horse went crazy with the band. The family followed the Excelsior Band.

Lucy and I would have gone had we known about his death.

Lucy also told me about a retired pilot friend of hers who started a small business flying people over Tampa Bay. He got a special request, to spread a man's ashes in the Bay. The pilot said, "I'm your man. Yes, I am." In flight they opened the window and pointed the urn in the right direction . . . or so they thought. The ashes came blowing back in the man's face. As they laughed the guy told the pilot that his friend had a great sense of humor and would have loved it. The pilot spent six months getting ashes out of his plane.

Did you know Wal-Mart, as of fall 2009, is selling caskets online? Don't they advertise "Save money? Live better"? How about "Save money. Die cheaper"? Wonder if they ever "Roll Back" those casket prices?

44

Fun With Did You Know?

What do old people and teachers have in common? They both love to give advice. This is good stuff I learned from experience and other people.

- When you clean out the dishwasher, put in detergent. If there is detergent, the dishes are dirty.
- Putting matching utensils in the same slot makes putting away easier.
- Get three estimates and references before making expensive car or appliance repairs.
- Get a second opinion before surgery.
- Plan a regular girls night out, be it a book, knitting or dinner club.
- When life seems unfair, ask God what He is trying to teach you.
- When you get paid, pay yourself first and put some into savings.
- Use credit cards carefully or not at all.
- Don't let friends tell you what to buy or do.
- Men may come and go, but a dog will love you forever, cats whenever.
- Develop a five year plan. To accomplish goals, plan ahead and stick to your plan.

- Don't leave a job before you have a new one.
- Travel as much as your budget, health and time allow.
- Create your own happiness.
- Make it a point to meet new people.
- Make friends who bring out the best in you.
- Save time to do the things you enjoy like art, photography, reading, etc.
- Turn off electronic stuff—live a little.
- Nothing is as important as family and friends.
- Criticize less, compliment and encourage more.
- Be kind—remember the Golden Rule.
- Don't waste your time on people who don't like you. You answer to God, not them.
- Okay, so it's your boss. Figure out what you can do to kiss up. (Sometimes a bottle of their favorite booze does it. It did for me.)
- Friends are God's gift to you. Stay in touch or reconnect.
- Don't be a slob; clean up after yourself.
- Break bad habits like smoking, drugs, drinking or eating too much.
- Help children to develop a good self image.

ADVICE FOR SINGLES

If you're seeking a long time relationship, think about internet dating. Writer/widow Valerie Frankle, over forty with two daughters, found her new husband through the internet. She interviews him for the male viewpoint at the end of her novel "The Girlfriend Curse".

Before you hop in the sack, show your interest in the person by asking questions to see if you share common values.

Long time married couples seem to all share similar family and cultural backgrounds.

The most important key to a good life is having the right partner. The person you choose is the most important decision you'll ever make. They hold the key to your emotional and financial future, and maybe your children's as well.

- Prepare for the worst, but plan for the best.
- Get as much education as you can.

- Ask your dentist what you should do with an after hour emergency. Friday afternoon to Monday morning is a long time to be in pain.
- Reach out to others. Speak up; shyness never got anyone anywhere, but try to be a class act. Or maybe be the class clown like me. I do have fun.
- Stop being negative toward yourself and others. Appreciate all good things in life, including the person you are.
- You will sleep better by avoiding caffeine after 2 o'clock and skip the 11 o'clock news.
- Be true to yourself without stepping on others.
- Look for someone to share your life, not just your bed.
- Think, think, and think before getting pregnant. A baby is a lifetime commitment. They are very demanding and self centered.
- Parents of teenagers need to know that they will eventually get easier to live with if you haven't spoiled them. (They get better after 30.)
- Turn off or ignore everything else when you're having a conversation with others, especially your child.
- Plan family sit down dinners without TV.
- Don't answer the phone during dinner.
- Kids will remember good times spent with you, not the gifts you bought.
- Teach your kids good table manners, the value of a handmade gift, to be caring and thoughtful, to write thank you notes, and how to manage money.
- When you say or do something stupid, ask for forgiveness.
- Trust in God and the inner you.
- Sometimes in life you're the bug and sometimes you're the windshield.
- Don't get your panties in a wad. Hold onto them and HAVE FUN!

45

Fun in the Kitchen?

The whole idea of cooking is ugly, ugly, ugly, since I hate it! After all, the word "cook" is a four-letter word, as I have heard. (Maybe Phyllis Diller?) I love to entertain by having bridge parties or even big buffet dinners. Hubby prefers having only one other couple at a time. The day-to-day, year-to-year cooking is boring, boring, boring to me. I also find that standing is very tiring. I would rather clean up after twenty dogs than fix a meal. When I am home alone I eat a lot of yogurt and cereal, or homemade soup and slaw. Canned V-8 and Slim-Fast or TV dinners also are fine for me. I would rather iron, clean house, pull weeds, clean toilets, bathe dogs, or fold clothes than cook.

Hubby loves to watch the TV food shows. I enjoy the HGTV decorating shows and movies. I seem to get really hungry watching those food shows. It becomes really irritating because I seem to be on a constant diet and they cook goodies.

My favorite thing to make is reservations. (Author unknown). True, true, true. I can cook. However, I used to be better at it. Hubby knows dinner is ready when our smoke alarm goes off.

At least I had the smarts to teach our two sons how to cook. Surprisingly they both love to cook. They are much better cooks than I. I'm not a bad cook, but I would rather fix the easy stuff. It doesn't help that I am allergic to lots of foods. I usually cook when Hubby is home.

My friend Randy (former co-worker in the decorating business) recently reminded me of the time I needed a new oven. He remembered a dinner party I had and my coming through the doors to the living room with smoke floating out all around me. He said I reminded him of the old Loretta Young (An "A" list movie star in the forties) TV show. In the opening scene Loretta floated through open doors. Randy is just so funny. I do remember the smoke while having a party—and being embarrassed. And yes, I had narrow double doors between my kitchen and living-dining room.

Randy also made me think about the time he was at our house when I had "gone on strike." The dishwasher had died. I continued to cook, but just rinsed off the dishes and put them in the sink. Finally I ran out of dishes, so I decided to soak them in my washing machine. There were just too many for the sink. Because Randy was there and I was distracted, I forgot to turn it off. Next thing we heard was very LOUD BANG, BANG, BANG, CRUNCH, CRUNCH, CRUNCH! I had very few dishes left. (It is probably difficult for you to believe I ever got A's in graduate school.)

Out I went and bought two sets of attractive, yet inexpensive, everyday dishes. They looked great with my expensive wallpaper. A few days later I finally got Hubby out to buy a new, low-end dishwasher on a "three-month, same as cash" deal. This was during our <u>very lean</u> years in Roswell, Georgia. We had two always-hungry teenage boys, a big mortgage, and no doubt, too many dogs. We bought a large brick ranch home with a daylight basement and one acre. We had qualified with my teaching income and Hubby's engineering pay. However, we had a separate contract on the remaining seven acres of our property. We had to replace the furnace soon after we bought the place. It was very difficult financially until we paid off our second mortgage which lasted for fifteen years.

In order to stretch money I got creative in the kitchen. With two rapidly growing boys that ate like gorillas, I gradually added dry milk to whole milk, finally getting it to half and half. I made all kinds of casseroles and soups. We had a lot of chili and spaghetti with day old bread. If we had any leftovers we had what we called "garbage soup" (now I call it "Yum Yum soup".)You add a can or two of soup and equal amounts of water, then add salt and pepper. To this, we would add grilled cheese sandwiches.

Here are some of our "Then and Now recipes." Most of you know that one can in a receipe—meaning the standard ones you see "LOTS of" at the grocery store. (They range from 14.5 to 16 ounce.)

Bean Soup (Full of beans—It's good!)

3 cans of black beans or northern beans
1 can of diced tomatoes
¾ pound of pulled pork (from your favorite restaurant)
½ jar of Paul Newman's mild salsa
½ cup chopped onions and/or peppers, if so desired

I buy a pound or two of pulled pork, some coleslaw, baked beans, and cornbread at my favorite Bar-B-Q restaurant. I have a meal with this combo, and then, with the leftover pork, I make the soup. I serve coleslaw and cornbread with the soup. Pretty tricky? Easy too!

Chili—(Huge pot)

1½ to 2 pounds of low-fat hamburger
2 cans of kidney beans
2 cans of diced tomatoes
1 jar of Paul Newman's mild salsa or chili seasoning
1 can of condensed tomato soup
1 cup of water
(Add 2 cups of water and 2 cans of tomato soup for a large crowd.)
1 large chopped onion (You can save some for top garnish.)
½ red pepper—if desired
½ yellow pepper—if desired

Cook hamburger and onions in a skillet and drain. Put ingredients in a LARGE pot. Bring chili to a boil. Then cook for at least an hour on low heat. Longer is better. This tastes better the more times you heat it up. I like it with slaw and, if possible, cornbread or half an English muffin. If you have six to eight hungry people, you might add grilled cheese sandwiches. I serve my awesome brownies (recipe also included) when I entertain a group.

Scalloped Potatoes Meal

1 package of scalloped potato mix (Follow directions, except use about half the milk and half the water.)

1 can diced tomatoes, drained

3 hot dogs, cooked and cut up (or sausage, pulled pork, or leftover ham)

1-1½ cups frozen peas

Put in oven on 325-350° F for 25-30 minutes. I like to serve with coleslaw or salad. If you are feeding it to a growing family, you may want to add corn bread or rolls. This is a perfect size for 4 people. Hubby and I usually make three meals out of it.

Baked Beans

2 large cans or 3 regular size cans of baked beans

½ cup brown sugar

½ cup of catsup (If beans have a lot of liquid, you may want to add less.) a small onion, if you like.

Place in a greased casserole dish, bake in the oven for 25-30 minutes at 325° F.

For Parties

I serve baked beans, along with cottage cheese (2 quarts) mixed with 1 can of crushed pineapple, sprinkled with paprika on top.

Then, to a dish of applesauce (a large glass gar), I sprinkle cinnamon on top.

I buy a cooked sliced ham that I bake. I serve it with whole wheat buns and a relish tray. (Celery, carrots, etc., plus mustard, mayonnaise, and pickles) and serve buffet style.

For dessert I may add my favorite easy Nestlé's Chocolate Chip Cookies or their oatmeal raisin cookies. You get these in the refrigerator department of your grocery store. At Christmas, I add some favorite family cookie recipes.

Cranberry Pecan Jell-O Salad or Dessert

(Often requested for covered-dish dinners. Use large, oblong dish.)

2 packages Jell-O (cranberry or raspberry)
2 cups of boiling water
1 cup of cold water
1 can of whole cranberries
2 cups of pecan pieces

Mix together and put in refrigerator for 6-8 hours. That's it, kids. (Hope you like it as much as my family and friends do.)

Awesome Brownies

I usually get 2 mixes, follow directions, adding about 1 cup of walnuts or pecans. Allow to cool. Sometimes I use prepared icing. However, my family prefers my old recipe. (I got it from the 4-H cooking booklet when I was twelve.) I ice the brownies and add lots of chopped nuts on top. Since these goodies are so high in calories I make them only a couple of times a year. If any are left, I separate and freeze them immediately so I won't overindulge.

Cocoa Icing

1 box of confectioners' sugar (sift to avoid lumps)—Don't we wish we could <u>sift our lumps</u>!
5-6 Tablespoons of cocoa (sift). Use more cocoa if you want.
1 stick of margarine (Leave out for about an hour since it needs to be soft.)
1 teaspoon of vanilla flavoring

Mix and spread over cooled brownies. Sprinkle a cup of chopped nuts. Enjoy!

These recipes are ones I use more often than I should. Note that they contain sodium, calories, preservatives, etc. They are good, but maybe not good for you. At my age I need all the preservatives I can get. (Old joke) If you only eat these foods occasionally and watch the portion sizes and exercise, they PROBABLY won't kill you—Standing over a hot stove—MAYBE.

Advice to moms—teach those kids to cook nutritious meals. (There are super kids' cookbooks to start them or you off.) Teach kids to iron a shirt, make up a bed, sort and do laundry without overloading machines. Teach them how to be responsible with money and how to use and balance a check book and use credit properly. Please teach them about protected sex and, boys especially, to use deodorant. Teach them to appreciate our world, God and everything that God gives them. Teach them to aim high and work for dreams to come true. Then someday you will have grown up kids who are very responsible members of their communities that you will be very proud of. If I did it, you can too!

46

Fun Playing Bridge

You know you're old when you walk into the senior center and you're not looking for your mama. Our friend Faye asked Hubby and me to join her at the senior center. (I might add—the most expensive friend I've ever had, since we ended up buying a home in North Carolina after she loaned us her house for a weekend.) We really enjoy playing bridge at the senior center, as we play four hands, with winners moving up. It's not as much fun playing for money since it becomes serious and it makes some old ladies crazy. You get the idea they can't eat without that three dollar win.

Hubby, who is a very bright, could be a top player if he played more often. There are a lot of very intelligent people who play, and then there is me. At my age I am being realistic. I'm a decent player, but I'm usually in the middle of the pack.

One of the couples we play with in North Carolina is Helena and Melvin. A few years ago Faye started calling Melvin, "Mean Melvin." He is a fun guy and a formidable player. Now a lot of us call him Mean Melvin. He has blue twinkly eyes, a happy attitude, and a wild sense of humor.

One day Hubby and I were late to bridge. Melvin's table was getting ready to start. He and his wife were partners. They spoke to me as I passed by them. I said, "How are you today, Mean Melvin?" He grinned and told me it was his birthday. I said, "How old are you, Mean Melvin?" "Twenty-nine." "Sure," I said. "No, really, how old are you?" He said,

"Eighty-six." I said, "Gee, Melvin, I thought you were older." Everyone loved it, especially Mean Melvin.

Actually, he could pass for 10 years younger. I told him I didn't bring a cake, but I brought some cookies. Later on he approached my table while eating an oatmeal cookie. He said, "Did you make this oatmeal cookie?" "Yes." "I thought I bit into a raisin, but it turns out it was a fly." I quickly said, "Oh good, I caught that sucker!"

Then Melvin asked me how I can be so fast and be so bad. I said, "I am younger and smarter." He said, "And uglier too." I said, "Yeah, that too." We all laughed.

A month later he was sitting at my table and taking forever to bid. I said, "Mean Melvin, get off your butt and bid." My bridge partner threw me a real dirty look. She is a lovely lady, but maybe sometimes is "too nice." Melvin told her, "That's all right, I like my women bad." (He does "get me," but isn't it funny how I seem to only remember "getting him"?)

Another time he was walking around with his pants falling below his waist. I said, "Gee, Melvin, if your pants fall any farther south, we're going to be able to see if you are a boxer or a brief kind of guy." His fun wife heard me and said, "Emily, I have been after him for years to pull his britches up." He later came over to play at my table and acted like he was mooning me. I said, "Wow, Melvin, I can see through your polo shirt. You really are a briefs guy." Melvin laughed and blushed. To get an older guy to blush is really cool. He tells people it's alright as he and Helena love me.

Another one of my favorite bridge buddies in North Carolina is Charles. He has that great British type of dry humor. I hear he is very good to his English-born wife. I'm sure that with his severe arthritis, their lives can't be easy. Thank goodness Charles hasn't lost his sense of humor or that twinkle in his eyes.

One day when we were partners, I bid incorrectly. (I hate "no trump" and avoid it.) He opened with one club, which usually means it is the best of the minor suits. That usually means the person wants his partner to mention their best major. I bid both majors, hearts and spades. Maybe diamonds (a minor suit) as well. I had no clubs. Charles bid seven clubs. I was about to die, knowing we'd go down, down, down. And I realized it was my fault for not bidding "no trump." I had gobs of points, and it turned out he had seven or eight top clubs. I put my cards on the table as I apologized for my bidding. Charles looked at my cards and said, "Kissy, kissy, hug, hug." We had all the top cards between us. He played it to perfection. This group has some really skilled and fun players! I love people with great wit, don't you?

I hope to meet his wife someday. One day Charles told us it was his wife's birthday. I asked him what he was going to give her. (He has rheumatoid arthritis. That's why I find his answer so funny.) "Well," he said, "I gave her three choices, the first being a therapeutic massage class, the second a lawn mower, and the third was dinner out at a nice restaurant in Asheville." He added, "Surprise, surprise, she chose the third." I said, "That's it?" He gave me a look and said, "Well, maybe I'll get her the lawn mower too." I think she does most of the yard work since it would be difficult for him. I hear he finances his wife's trips back to England so she can see the queen (only joking) and her relatives.

He and a fine gentleman, Pelham, were partners. Priscilla was my partner. Priscilla said, "Show Charles what your Hubby gave you for your big birthday (70th)." Extending my hand I showed Charles my small but wonderful diamond cocktail ring that rotates. (Normally I receive a $30-$40 gift. So you know it was a big birthday.) Charles looked at it and his eyes widened. He said, "What would you do if some guy tried to rip it off your finger?" Immediately I said, "I would kick him in the b***s." I couldn't believe I said that, but I did. Fortunately they all laughed.

Pelham is so cute. He has a twinkle about his face and very expressive eyes. He reminds me so much of my dad. A fun, fun gentleman with a wonderful dry sense of humor. He is an excellent bridge player, as is Joyce. She is always fun and is patient with me. I'm sure it isn't easy for really good players like them to be my partner. I like bridge, but I don't want to play more than once a week. Some of my friends, like Faye, play four or five times a week. They are going to be better because of all the practice and most are smarter people than I am. I feel it is a "game" and should be <u>enjoyed</u>. Some people are so serious. Honestly, they should play only competitive championship bridge players. I'm glad our group is into "fun bridge."

On one of our cruises Hubby and I played with a couple from England. Man, were they good. Turns out they play five or six times a week. Instead of saying "Pass" they say "No bid" (said really fast). I had to ask them twice what they were saying. I found that interesting.

I like "party bridge" because you don't get stuck with the same four people for hours at a time. Frankly, I get bored. (Surprise, surprise, surprise!) One time I was a substitute in a marathon group. We started at

12:30 or 1:00 and played until 5:00. All were much better players than I. But no one wants to feel like they are the poorest at anything. Not only did I think I was the worst, I knew it! In this group you played with one table of four and NEVER changed partners. I love party bridge, when you play four hands and move. That way you get to talk and play with most of the people. Surprise, it's even better with dessert.

47

Fun with Sex

Shame on you if this is the first chapter you read. I hate to ask anyone for help, but I had to in order to write this chapter. My sex life has not been that interesting. (I didn't say it hasn't been wonderful, honey.) My story will probably be boring to you, since I was a virgin until I married at 23. I have never strayed. I never said I haven't been tempted or haven't lusted, OK? I believe that marriage vows should be taken seriously.

I like to talk and joke about sex. Whenever some young person wants to tell me something about his or her sex life, I ask them if they want to hear about mine. That shuts them up.

I've heard some incredible and amusing <u>true</u> sex stories from others. How about the couple who went camping and came back with poison ivy: hers on the inside of her thighs, his on his face. You figure it out.

I know a gal who had a very active sex life with her much older husband. When he began to experience problems he asked her to go to his doctor with him. As it happened, his doctor was a <u>former high school classmate of HERS</u>. The doctor explained to them that as a man gets older he needs variety. She got defensive, saying, "I'll have you know I've been a good wife. We've done it on the back of a pickup, on a roof that started to cave in, in an elevator, on a beach and in all kinds of places and all kinds of positions." Stunned, the doctor said, "I can't believe you did all that."

Another friend of mine married a guy 25 years older. In his eighties, they still had passionate sex twice a week. He lifts weights and stays in condition to keep up—and keep it up, apparently. She told me that when they first got together, he told her to tell him where and what turned her on. Due to his severe hearing loss from World War II she had to speak loudly hoping the neighbors wouldn't hear. One day this couple was out skinny-dipping in his lake. One thing led to another when all of a sudden they heard a friend calling his name by the shore. It was a very embarrassing experience for my modest girlfriend.

Another friend told me that after her wedding she couldn't stop crying as she hugged her Dad goodbye. Her dad told her she didn't have to go. She told him she was married and she had to go. She cried for miles. A day or two later, on their way to California, she had another BIG problem: constipation. She finally told her husband. When they stopped for gas, he purchased a package of Ex-Lax and told her to take the whole package! Yum, yum, yum. Then she had the opposite problem. Sometimes life is not easy and can be downright embarrassing.

Before marriage he had told his fiancée that he had a neat apartment, cool furniture and a pool. Turns out ALL the furniture was purchased for $500—including a FEATHER center piece. Not the luxury look she was expecting.

She told us about the pretty, blue, satin sheets the big guy bought. I said, "No doubt to match your baby blue eyes!" Then my friend tells us that in the throes of passion they slid off the bed. Surprise, surprise, surprise!

One of my Dal pals lives in a large central Florida retirement community with several golf courses. With golf, card games, excursions, etc., etc.! A person could fill up every hour of every day of the week. He invited us to his home for drinks. We saw it all while getting lost. I told Hubby I could see myself living there, however it was "too organized" for him. It does have the "roach motel" factor. People checking in, but seldom leave standing up. It contains a large hotel where big bands frequently perform. I could picture Hubby and me going there having fun, eating and dancing.

Recently I have heard from two excellent sources that there have been times on Saturday nights when mayhem occurs. It seems that some of the gals toss keys to their rented rooms on the table. The guys grab a key and see what they get. The male enhancement pills go to work. Some have died from heart attacks. This isn't easy for the little lady left at home to hear. Can you imagine a son or daughter asking Mom why she seems to be "so damn mad" at Dad? Or the grandchild who asks, "How did Granddad die?" I would cut "it" off and send "it" to the other woman if I found out who she was. (Message here is: Don't mess with me or my man.) This county also has the largest incidence of venereal diseases. Maybe you young folks need to get some condoms for your grandparent's birthday. What do you think?

Another friend's older father-in-law (80+) had a heart attack caused by sex enhancement pills. It can and does happen, but luckily he recovered. Sex is probably more fun for older women if you are a cougar. "Younger" sounds more interesting. However, if I were single I wouldn't want to get naked in front of anyone. NO! NO! NO! My ears still look good, that's about it.

Did you know that when a woman reaches a climax, the powerful hormones released make the woman want to bond with the man? Wonder how professionals deal with this? I have a girl friend that gets to know a guy very well before "doing it." Once that happens, she goes from a confident woman to a "clinging vine" type. Then the guy backs off.

To women, sex is not about mechanics. Foreplay to a woman is a man's attitude and behavior. Hey, men (if you happen to sneak a peek at this book), if you are a jerk and piss off your sweetie the LAST thing she will want is sex. Right, women?

I hear most guys are into warm bodies and a good time. With all the disease and loosening of standards, if I were young I'd be concentrating on a career. As a nun? No, I'm not Catholic so that wouldn't work. Years ago a friend told me she thought having the guy get HIV tested and get a financial report on the guy was the way to go.

If you are with an older guy you might want to tell him that a guy told me that Pabst Blue Ribbon Beer works better than Viagra.

Just remember, somewhere someone is probably having unprotected sex. Hope it isn't your Grandpa—or anyone you know.

Chelsea Handler has a problem, as I do, with teen girls deliberately getting pregnant. She said, "It is stupid, and if a girl can't put on a condom she shouldn't be getting laid." I agree.

I'm just glad I am married to a working nerd. But "singles," it is better to be single than to be in a bad marriage. So think long and hard before you take the big step. I can tell you men don't get better with age. They just get old along with you. Marriage isn't easy.

48

Fun with Shoes and Bags

No, not old bags (like me), but handbags.

Jean Bice, of QVC fame said, "You never can have too many friends or shoes." However, due to back challenges, I can no longer wear high heels. I still love them and you tell me what woman doesn't love bags.

I recently met a cute twenty year old that had on to-die-for shoes. They had a black patent platform with zebra stripe straps. How cute! So was she! I told her if I had thought I could wear them I would have wrestled her to the floor over them. Every day I notice Kelly Ripa's heels on "Regis and Kelly." Do you?

The first shoes I remember were white high top oxfords before graduating to brown oxfords. The only neat shoes I had growing up were the ones grandma Ada bought me when I was ten. All the other little girls were wearing black patent Mary Jane's like Shirley Temple wore in the movies. My Daddy said no, I couldn't have them. However, when I went to visit grandma Ada got me a pair. I may have mentioned I wanted some, but I was taught not to ask for things. Since she had ten grandchildren, and not much money, we never were given a lot. This made it extra special, but I was her first grandchild.

A few days later I wore my new shoes when Aunt Mary took me to Cleveland to a really nice department store for lunch. Up until the nineties, big department stores all had lovely dining rooms. I was so impressed, as

I never ate out except on one family vacation. I remember she asked me what I wanted for dessert. I said I didn't want anything, thank you, after seeing the prices. In my mind I didn't think she should spend her money buying me an expensive dessert. However she said she was going to have one and wanted to get me one. That chocolate cake was so good. I had been three when she and Uncle Francis got married, and apparently they really liked me.

Aunt Mary and Uncle Francis had two sons, Lowell and Claire. (My most ornery cousins.) When Aunt Mary was older she had both breast removed from cancer. Sometime later I went to see her. When I hugged her I could feel all the bones in her chest as well as her bony back. I was very concerned. She died two days later. My Aunt Emily was convinced she waited to see me before she died.

When I was thirteen, due to the curvature of the spine, I had to go to an orthopedic doctor. He prescribed the ugliest shoes. The shoe store heated up the arch of the shoe. (How, I do not know.) When I put them on, the warm shoe molded to my foot. They were the ultimate arch supports. My grandmothers both had more attractive oxfords than I. Get this, mine were "dog doo" brown, with wing tips and little tiny holes and small heels. They were very expensive. Being a teenager with acne and lots of bad hair days plus ugly shoes was not fun. Thank you God for my sense of humor, a lot of friends, and a loving family.

World War II had ended, but there wasn't much available in shoes and clothing. I remember waiting in the family car while the ugly shoes were repaired.

When I got to high school somehow my mother, who also loved shoes, was able to get me a pair of sandal oxfords that I loved. I would put on the old lady comforts for all my chores. I actually kept the ugly shoes for 12 years until Hubby and I moved to Florida and my feet got wider. I know that somehow feet sizes change in Florida.

I recall when I was going to the junior prom how panicked my mother and I were over shoes. We finally found some size ten black ballet type shoes. They weren't that lovely and they hurt my feet, but I was happy to have them.

When I was a senior in high school I worked Saturdays from 9am to 9pm at a shoe store. It was tiring for a flat footed teen. They were no removable arch supports. I was able to get a pair of red high heels sandals and at that time and a pair of black leather high heel pumps. Did I ever think I was hot stuff!

After Hubby and I were married and living in Hartford, Connecticut, I was able to order a lovely pair of navy pumps. When we moved to St. Petersburg, Florida, I was so excited when "Peltz Shoe Store" opened as they specialized in hard to fit sizes at reasonable prices.

We soon moved to Clearwater, but a couple of times a year I would go to St. Petersburg to Peltz. This was the start of my obsession with shoes.

In 1964 I received a neat catalog from Capezio. They specialized in ballet shoes and some neat flats. I saved my money and bought a pair that had square toe, throat, and a very small square heel and were black velvet. Some forty years later I still wear them for Christmas events and cruises. Believe it or not they still look good. As I have gotten older my feet have stretched so now the shoes are a bit short. If I were going to be buried I would be buried with them. Is that sick?

Now I am lucky to have lots of shoes thanks to catalogs. It seems kind of ridiculous in that I wear running shoes with extra arch supports or my acupuncture arch rubber flip-flops. I started wearing these types of flip-flops in the early seventies. I had a bone spur on my heel which I got rid of by wearing them. Be careful breaking them in, wear socks with them for 5 minutes, gradually increasing in time worn. (Masseys.com or 1-800-627-7379.) Hubby had a bone spur at the same time. His doctor gave him a shot and prescribed expensive arch supports.

Handbags are fun to have in several colors. We used to wear matching shoes and bags. Now we often wear bags for a pop of color, like the French.

My generous friend Sandy has given me a couple of nice bags. She has about a zillion. Ok, so I exaggerate, but she does have a special closet for her collection. She even has some of those fancy-dancy ones that come with matching billfolds. I can't imagine changing my wallet so often. I still use my shiny vinyl leopard one I have had for a few years. If I had more than one I would probably lose it, like my head—if it wasn't attached.

Storage for shoes and bags can be a problem. I store mine in a clear, divided shoe bag mounted on the back of my closet door and the adjoining wall. My handbags are hanging on a white antique bentwood hall tree behind my bedroom door. Limited storage forces me to pass them on. If they bring joy to others, it brings joy to me.

My catalog shoe sources are: Maryland Square.com or 1-800-727-3895 and Old Pueblo Traders 1-800-362-8400.

49

Fun Around Town

Love, love, love small towns and the people who live in them. It's fun to run into people you know or recognize. Our Florida home is located in a small, non-gated neighborhood. When the houses were being built, my husband and I met everyone. Since we purchased a place in North Carolina and are gone four months at a time, we don't often see our Florida neighbors. Darn.

Before we had our home built, I checked out some of the neighbors. One cute couple I called Mr. and Mrs. Puff Puff. Both heavy smokers, first one would puff and then the other. Soon after we met, Mrs. Puff Puff died suddenly. Maybe too soon—Mr. Puff Puff met a curvaceous brunette who was visiting him every weekend. A bit shocking. Turns out his stepdaughter introduced him to the new woman. She didn't want her stepdad to move back to Virginia. With the wisdom of age, I now understand that men who have had good marriages are likely to remarry sooner. (I told my Hubby, "DO NOT think about doing that for at least a year, or I'll haunt you.")

One day I was teasing Mr. Puff Puff, and he laughed and said, "If you weren't married and I wasn't getting married, I would chase after you."

In his face, I said "If you were the LAST MAN on the planet—forget it!"

He laughed.

A few months later, they announced they were getting married. We were all invited to the lovely outdoor wedding (fewer than six months after his wife's death). The beautiful wedding was held in his sweeping backyard with about sixty relatives, friends, and neighbors. After the wedding Mr. Puff Puff served champagne with strawberries and cream. He had told the "hottie" to just show up. He had planned the whole thing on his own. What a classy guy.

He had asked me if I had any small tablecloths. I made some for him to use. After the late afternoon wedding, we were invited to a local steak restaurant. We were to order anything off the menu. After dinner Mr. Puff Puff announced that we were all going out on an old sailing ship. One of the guys played a harmonica, and we sang songs as we enjoyed the balmy ocean breezes.

Two years later, the newlyweds moved to a townhouse. They both loved boating, and from then on we didn't see or hear from them. Recently, 10 years later, I ran into the "hottie," and we planned to meet that evening for dinner. We had a fun time reminiscing.

Our "favorite neighborhood guy" is just the cutest "younger brother" we all wish we had. When I was getting ready to go to the mountains, I gradually pack up my van. It takes me a week. I don't want to forget anything . . . and, I always take too much stuff. My dog, her crate, her meds, grooming supplies, food, leads, water bowls, etc., and my art supplies, plants, books, my clothes, etc. etc. etc. One day this neighbor said, "Hey Emily, I wish you would hurry up and go, so I could start missing you." Wasn't that just too cute?

In each small town I have my friends. They are the book club gals, the bridge gals, guys and gals in my writers' club and art groups. I have always been a joiner. Years ago I was vice president of the Clearwater, Florida, American Association of University Women, and later on, the president of the Roswell, Georgia, A.A.U.W. I was involved in the Junior Women's Club in California. Years later I was a member of the local Woman's Club. For years I was active in the Atlanta Kennel Club. I helped found two regional Dalmatian clubs. All these activities were fun, and most took place in small towns.

One of the most interesting small-town experiences I've ever had was in Los Altos, California, (mid-'60s). Unfortunately, I don't always open my mail every day. If I think something is not important, it sits there a while. Apparently I need my clutter. Yes, I know, you open all your mail tossing catalogs and junk mail as you walk through your garage. I know you take care of everything immediately and have neat and tidy files. Your home is probably neat and tidy too. Well, goody-goody for you. Unfortunately, I keep a clean, but not very organized home.

A letter addressed to me had arrived from the Methodist church. I put it aside and didn't open it until two or three weeks later. Hey, I was busy! I taught school, had a husband, two sons, and a house to care for; graduate classes; and A.A.U.W., Junior Women, and church activities. So give me a break. My life was full, yet fun. Finally, after about two weeks, I opened the letter. Shock, shock, shock! I read: "If we don't hear from you in 10 days we will assume you agree to be a member of the Church Missionary Committee."

WOW! A pretty smart minister, I'm thinking. How hard can this be? The missions are in Africa, right? We probably collect clothes, shoes, and canned goods.

Wrong, wrong, wrong! The mission was another church—and not even Methodist. It was a Catholic church. When I was growing up, Methodist was good, Quaker was good, Baptist and Presbyterians were OK, but Catholic was difficult to understand because I had a problem with their concept of confession. I now realize that in the "Dark Ages," parents and teachers (if there were any) weren't on Earth to listen to kids. The kids were there to listen to ADULTS. The priest was/is perhaps an underpaid therapist. Many adults had no one else to go to. People worked very hard all day. They were tired. When it got dark, no lighting, so everyone went to bed. (Hey, MAYBE you should rethink your hard life.)

When I went to the Mission Committee meeting, I was still wondering why our mission was a Catholic church. This tiny church, just ten miles away, was growing and had lots of challenges with the congregation primarily of migrant Mexican workers. (These migrant workers were probably a lot like some my son knows of in South Florida. Almost slave labor, with HORRIBLE working and living conditions. Some animals (any of my dogs) have had much better lives. Our church, along with others in the community, came to their aid.

That mission was one of my many life experiences which made me aware of the value of working hard for a higher education. (I worked my way through college.) I am very thankful for ALL that God has allowed me: loving family, neat friends and a nice home, good food to eat, and more.

Think of how I ended up working over in Sunnyvale, helping people in that small congregation. For sure I wouldn't have volunteered. I honestly believe God puts us in situations (some can be dramatic—life or death) to teach us lessons. If something huge happens to you, ask yourself what God is trying to teach you. If you don't, I feel you are going to get more "lessons" thrown at you. You may want to read *The Game of Life and How to Play It*, by Florence Scovel Shinn. It helped me through some really tough spots. It contains lots of good affirmations and amazing, inspirational stories.

50

Fun with Joan Rivers

Joan Rivers, I remember your first appearance on the Tonight Show. Having done standup, I have some idea of how much crap you probably have gone through. Ever had a mic cut off while the audience seemed to love your "bit"? I have. Maybe we could do standup together. We could wear our classic matching red "Joan Rivers" jackets over our black outfits. It would be funny since I am tall and you're such a little thing.

Maybe before our "big event" we could go and get our roots done. Hey girlfriend, if I were a big "TV deal" like you, I would get mine done more often

A side story about your/my red jacket that I love almost as much as my J.R.'s black leopard lined trench coat: my very attractive, much younger, writer friend Marla borrowed the jacket from me. Marla is a very smart business woman, but she forgot to bring something nice to wear to our annual Florida Writer's Conference dinner. It was a size too large, but Marla looked great in it! She would look good in a paper bag since she has yet to outgrow her looks. The NERVE of that girl. She asks me if I mind if she orders one like it. Well she ends up with two-one in red and one in black. Can you believe? Joan, aren't you glad I'm your best friend?

Months later at a local writer's meeting I am wearing Joan River's white hoop earrings, a QVC yellow jacket with blue hydrangeas, a yellow tee and white pants. Marla loved the outfit and asked if I minded if she ordered the same. I said, "Okay, but I kinda hope they don't have the jacket in your size."

Recently I ordered a white jacket on sale (magic words to me) from N.M. Loved it, but it was a size too small. Guess who bought it and saved me return fees. She is becoming the daughter I always wanted. It would be nice to have ONE kid who listens to me. Does Melissa qualify? Joan, I never got to see your entire reality series. What I saw was fun. Joan, as adorable as my grandson was/is, yours is beautiful!

You need to know that I bought your good book "Men Are Stupid and, Like Big Boods" and your QVC sunglasses set. I had the dark red ones redone with prescription lenses. I get a lot of compliments on your/mine stuff. Maybe with my artsy fartsy clothing background, we ought to design a collection for neat old bitches like us. I know Marla would buy it.

That's it. No more kissing up for you Joanie.

51

Fun With This and That

Fun things keep happening—thank you God!

A sinus infection led me to another visit with Dr. Mountain Man. He can be funny, but maybe not as funny as he imagines.

He says, "Don't you think I'm ruggedly handsome?" I reply, "I don't know any woman who would think that!" As I am leaving, Dr. Mountain Man says, "See you later Dude." I say, "You can call me lady, woman, or bitch, but do NOT call me Dude."

I hear he plays in a rock band. Give me a break. Who wants to go see him play little finger cymbals?

I'm having more fun with eighty-eight year old "Mean Melvin". After he was giving me a rough time, I said, "Melvin, the ONLY reason you are still alive is because God wants me to continue to give you a rough time." He grins and says, "It's a good thing we love each other."

Recently I saw 97 year old Charlotte at our Mountain Friendship Club luncheon. She is so cute with her red bob, makeup and stylish clothes. Bless her heart, she's still bitching about her family taking away her car keys.

She said she feels the secret of her longevity is doing her own housework and playing Bridge. (She's still good at it too.) Charlotte and her little dog live across the road from her daughter. What a neat, inspiring, fun lady! P.S.—She knows how I am and still can't wait to read my book.

Last week I got "the roots" done. Alfredo and I were bitching about flying overseas. I was telling him I wanted to trip a toddler who, when he wasn't crying, was running up and down the aisles. Alfredo experienced a similar aggravation on his trip to Italy.

He said he asked the flight attendant to do something about it. The attendant told him he "wasn't allowed". Alfredo "lost it" because the child's mother was sleeping while the kid wasn't. So Alfredo woke her speaking loudly saying, "How dare you sleep when your kid is keeping me awake. If you don't make him behave, I'm going to put him back where he came from." With that, the Italian mother told Alfredo to "@%^&* off" and get his own plane. Alfredo's loud voice frightened the kid enough to make him stop causing any more problems.

I feel sorry for parents who have to travel with little ones. Most do behave, thank God. Maybe the airlines could put the toddlers in a closed off area where sprinkler systems could go off when they get out of control. Hey . . . spraying water in the face of "mouthy" dogs has always worked for me.

Advice to parents: do not take toddlers on planes unless it's <u>absolutely necessary</u>. It is NOT fair to the child and NOT fair to the other passengers who've spent their hard earned money. If you're "military" and <u>have</u> to do this, God bless you.

Advice to other parents: unless your kid can read a long book, leave him home alone or maybe with his grandma (unless she's like me).

Okay, I like kids when they can clean their own butts and can carry on an intelligent conversation—and don't scream—okay?

Did any of you see The New Yorker cartoon (7/4/11) where the baby bird, on a limb, is saying to his mama in the nest, "No need to push, Mother, I'm going." I maintain mothers come primarily in two types. "Mama Bird" who loves and encourages her kids to fly in life or "Mother Hens" who want those kids around forever. I love my kids, but I don't need to spend a great deal of time with them. I do love our phone chats! My grandson who's twenty-eight . . . . now that's different. Not only does he not scream, he is fun, Fun, FUN! Plus he is my favorite grandchild. When we're together I tell strangers this, and he says witty things like "the others got killed in an avalanche". People are shocked until we laugh. See what I mean? I love to spend one-on-one time with him. This usually happens around his birthday or Christmas. We love "our day". Often we go to brunch and shopping, usually for some special clothes he wants.

J.D. tends to like having a few very nice clothes. We always shoe shop for me, which is mostly a waste of time. We go to furniture stores where we imagine what he would buy if he were moving into his own home. His grandmother is trying to teach him about design as I discuss how some of my things would look with the things he likes. Hey, if daughter-in-love or sons don't want my "treasures", J.D. or my friends will.

My friend Brett wants my "Jean Harlow" chairs. I met Brett years ago at Rowland's Upholstery Shop while we were fabric shopping for our design clients. Brett also owns two of the top restaurants (Brett's and P.L.A.E.) on our island. At the bar he serves the best barbeque I've ever had. He's in his fifties, handsome, bright, a singer, a writer and one helluva lot of fun! He is also a fan of mine. He says he wants to have "a do" (southern, for party) for me when I launch this book. Other fans take note, especially those with restaurants.

Recently I was talking to a friend who told me she had to take a shower because the bug man was coming. I said, "Bugs in the bush?" The next time I talked with her she told me she had bugs in her pantry. I pretended not to hear well. "What kind of bugs are in your panties?" I ask.

My artist friend Pat's daughter's cat Zeke is quite a character. In order to get Moe up he pats the touchy/feely lamp, turning it on. If that doesn't work, he jumps on the dresser knocking off items one by one until she gets up. That's amusing unless you are Moe.

A friend told me she knows a couple that have a clap on/ clap off lamp. They got a surprise when in the heat of passion the light goes on and off. Wondering is the head board talking to the lamp?

If you have any funny decorating stories please email them to: emilyjoannehoover@gmail.com. and I will try to fit them into the next book, *Hold On To Your Panties and Decorating Too.*

52

Fun Being Blessed

God, as you now realize, has an everyday challenge with me. However, He has gotten me through some really tough times: cancer, kidney failure, and a horrible auto accident, just to mention a few.

Sometimes I can't believe the absolute joy I receive in one day. I had lunch with my art friend, Pat Mennenger, who is putting the finishing touches on art work for my book. We were having fun catching up on our lives when I overheard a girl nearby say, "She was kind of nice." I said, "I'm sorry, I heard that. That's so funny can I use it in my book?" I gave them my bookmark. They want me to come to Hendersonville for their book club. What fun!

After lunch I raced to Dr. See's office. I have to have my eye pressure checked. "Dr. Four-Eyes" in Florida feels he needs this four times a year to keep up with the glaucoma. I see Dr. See's assistant for my field vision test. I tell her she looks wonderful and ask her how she went from fluffly to fab. She gives me a flyer about some Zumba parties.

Lord helps me find the right exercise! Without Curves here, I have to do something. I know diet and exercise keep me going. So will I be going to Zumba? Everything becomes such a BIG DEAL when you get older. All we want to do is rest, read and watch TV. Or, like Faye, drive or play bridge.

I go into Dr. See's exam room and spot a new, high style, interior design magazine that I love. I ask Dr. See, if I promise to bring it back, could I please take it home to copy something.

He said, "You can have it as there probably isn't anyone in town that would appreciate it as much as you."

Dr. See goes on to start a long conversation about the level of sophistication in our town. He tells me this is a "truck" town. He had a red truck and a Shelby Mustang. After he sold both, everyone asked him what happened to his truck. A vintage Shelby designed Mustang is worth a lot.

Dr. See tells me a joke. I tell him about "Dr. Four Eyes". We are giggling like school girls. Finally I ask, "Am I keeping you from another patient?" He tells me his last patient cancelled.

I should call him Dr. Funny, but that might not come off so good.

On the way home to feed Diva, "THE" Dalmation, I stop to say "hi" and get an appointment with my hairdresser, Alfredo. He introduces me to his client. By this time everyone is gone. He asks about the book as I give him some bookmarks. His client asks me if she can get one. I say, "You may not qualify". She asks why. I say, "It is only for bad ass girls. Are you one?" She says, "You bet your sweet ass I'm a bad ass girl." My, my. Guess I got told.

After taking care of "the Diva" I go down the mountain to meet Faye for dinner. Hubby is out of town. I had to wait on a red truck. I pull out behind it and we go a short distance before he turns right. I turn right, he turns left, and I turn left. Damn! He parks right where I always do. I lower my window as I park one space away. I say, "I hope you don't think I'm following you." "I'm here to meet a friend. Probably like you." He says, "I'm here to change my shorts." "Don't do it in front of me!" I quip.

It turns out he's a mere 18 years old. I ask him what he's going to do with his life. He seems very mature for his age, but I tell him he needs to do a lot of research before going into business. I advise taking as many business classes as possible and getting a lot of experience.

We see Faye coming. I double dare him to say "you are the hottest 85 year old I've ever seen". Faye gets out of her car and immediately says, "You trying to pick up this man Emily?" She turns to him and says, "I know her husband." Then bless his heart the young man says to Faye, "You are the hottest 85 year old I have ever seen." Laughing, Faye says,

"Emily put you up to that!" I replied, "Bet you never had so much fun with a couple of old ladies."

With a grin he says, "See ya."

I crack, "Only if you're lucky!"

I love cute teens. Faye rolls her eyes and says, "You have fun wherever you go."

Yes I do. Thank God!

When the media discovered a certain politician had a kid with the live-in maid, they went crazy with front page photos, etc.

I went crazy and called Helen. I told her that her mom and I had kept a secret and that this man and I had a one night stand and she was our love baby. Then I called a few more "younger" friends and told them the same thing. Hey, if you're not English major and get bored writing, you have to do something fun. I'm glad I don't text.

I live to hear laughter.

53

Fun in Europe 2011

Leaving late in the afternoon, Hubby, son T.J. and R.R. (his partner of over twenty years) and I flew from Miami to Berlin, Germany. Twelve hours cramped into short seats with our long legs touching the seats in front, and not being able to sleep was not easy for Hubby and me. It is a wonder we are still married. Traveling sorts out those that are committed to making the marriage work and those who are too selfish to try. If more couples would do this BEFORE marriage, it might change the divorce rate.

You have to learn to compromise in relationships. Ask yourself, is this really worth an argument? How important will it be in five years? It's not about who is right. You can be right and it will be hurtful or end your relationship. You can't take back harmful words.

We arrived in Berlin and raced to get a flight to Venice. My seatmate was a very interesting woman who I believe taught medicine. She also owned an art gallery. She was on her way to Venice to see a friend and to go to a big art show.

We drove into Venice from the airport where T.J. had rented us a car. We went an hour Northwest to stay three nights in a lovely old renovated stone mill. (website: http:www.ivecchimulin.it).

The rooms were super clean and they served a wonderful breakfast of juice, cereal, and fresh hot croissants. The owner's name was Fav. He was tall, in his forties, and very charming as he verbally attacked me every chance he got. Of course I held my own. We all had fun with him. His beautiful, curvy fiancee (in her late thirties) loved it when I told her she could do better. They were so cute.

They'd known each other three years and have common backgrounds. So this first marriage should be a good one.

It is not unusual for several generations to live together. Fav explained that his parents bought part of the mill twenty years ago and renovated it as their home. A few years later Fav bought the rest and had an architect design a home for him in the large structure, where he and fiancee live the rest into guest suites. His sister, and only sibling, lives in a stone house behind the mill. Fav says, "We like being close so we can look after one another." THAT was so sweet it was all I could do to refrain from vomiting.

Fav recommended we drive the 200 mile round trip to the lake region. It was raining, so we thought that was a good idea. T.J. and R.R. had slept on the plane and were ready to roll. Hubby and I had gotten a good night's sleep so we were "sort of" ready.

T.J. is a very experienced European driver, and we all loved the beautiful green expanse of the Italian countryside, the rolling hills and the flatlands. We saw quaint small towns and majestic mountains. The day was perfect with lunch beside the water at an open air restaurant. I even had time to buy a leopard scarf from a street vendor. The following day we visited some of the large gardens near the mill.

Way too soon we had to pack up and head to Venice to board our ship "The Voyager of the Seas".

If you've never cruised, you don't know what you are missing. It is a wonderful experience! I think it is sorta like going to summer camp when you're young. Lots of activities to choose from, like swimming, sun bathing or gambling. The cruise ships all have a game room for bridge etc. and a library where you can borrow or leave a book. There's an exercise room, a jogging track and a movie room. There are also programs for children. In addition, the cruise director is always planning something special. You travel to neat places, meet interesting people and you can eat all day and night. Plus every evening they provide great entertainment.

Old sailors take note: the larger ships are so stable there is seldom any sway. Ladies, you'll love sleeping "in", going to breakfast, and coming back to a spotless bath and neatly made bed. You unpack once, which makes life easier. What's not to love? If you get a "deal" through the internet, you can sometimes get an inside cabin for about $200 per person per day. Remember—food 24/7, your floating hotel, entertainment etc. Upgrades, like balcony rooms, which we like, are more. Booking either very early or very late will OFTEN get you better deals. We booked ahead.

I don't understand why so many people are not afraid to fly, but are afraid they'll drown. How many big ships have gone down in the last twenty years?

Our ship stopped in Koper, Slovevia, Ravenva and Bari, Italy. My favorite was Dubrovnik, Croatia, with its old buildings and narrow streets. Views of the city and sea were awesome from almost anywhere.

All along the Dalmatian coast little towns and big cities rose up from the sandy beaches. Small houses clung to the mountains.

Royal Caribbean provided some nice tours for those willing to rise early and pay the price. Hubby and I rented a taxi with a charming tour guide/driver. I loved our fifty or sixty mile tour of the small country. People there have gone through so much—defending their territory and fighting for independence. We saw bombed out buildings along the coast that were heartbreaking.

Hubby had a real challenge getting money from a bank machine so we could pay our driver. The exchange rate experience wasn't good, but he persevered. After arriving back near our ship, Hubby did his exploring walking and I went shopping. Yeah! About time, right?

There was an expensive tourist shop with lots of lovely things. I spotted some beautiful black and white silk ties embroidered with Dalmatian dogs. I would have loved to get my sons and grandson one, but way too pricey. I did find some small Dalmatian items that I thought my "bad ass" girlfriends would love.

This being the Dalmatian Coast, where Dalmatian dogs come from, I asked a couple of locals if they had seen any. The girl in the pricey shop said, "Yes." Several others I spoke to said no. I don't see how the poor dogs could get enough exercise as all the yards we saw were very, very small.

Hubby and I had a delightful lunch on an outside terrace overlooking the sea. We walked downstairs to see "old town". After a short time I left him to explore on his own, which he enjoyed.

Speaking of exercise . . . . on our trip, mine was walking from the dining room to the acupuncturist and to the entertainment.

Unfortunately a few days before our trip I "did something" to cause my hip to act up. This made any walking a challenge. Walking up and downstairs and on cobblestones is NOT something I could do without pain. I had gone to an acupuncturist and a chiropractor twice before our trip.

The acupuncturist on the ship was a real cutie. He warned against going ashore the next day because of the strenuous terrain. I decided to stay on board, to rest, and to work on the "damned book".

The "boys" left early. Hubby decided to go see Bari on his own. Bari looked to me like a big industrial city. I wasn't thrilled he was going by himself. I was, however, happy to have a day to myself.

I did some writing while having lunch at one of the outside courts. Later I moved to a quiet table and spent the rest of the afternoon writing. Around five o'clock I decided to have some fun. I called Hubby from the spa. (Cell phones don't work on ships.) He was back and happy to join me for a glass of wine. Meanwhile, I found a couple of loungers for us, put my bag on one and waited for him to arrive.

Before long I saw a very curvaceous, brunette who I'd guess was in her late forties. This classy gal was something! She was wearing a smart black v-neck swimsuit with a white gauze cover-up that wasn't doing its job. She was very well endowed. She asked if the other lounger next to me was taken. "No, please join me," I replied.

Ann was a remarkable woman. She told me that she has been in Europe on vacation for two months—alone. She lives in Southern California and owns a tea room that was written up in Forbes Magazine. Wow!

Because of some unusual medical problems, her doctor insisted she get away from her business pressures and let her body heal. My new friend and I had so much fun chatting. At some point I told Ann that my daddy would have said, "That girl's dumplings are boiling over." Women, if you have the "girls" showing, people can't help but notice. Ann laughed and told me that whenever she is in Hollywood strange women would come up and ask who "did" them. They can't believe they're natural. I should have told her to enjoy them before she's tripping over them.

Ann told me about her sweet, but nosey, mom who just happened to look in her night stand. Her mom asked her how she used Pepper for sex. Ann laughed and explained that she put it on her salad. She likes to eat in bed and watch television.

When she told me she was twice a widow, I responded, "I hope of natural causes."

She told me she was on a repeat cruise, having taken the same one the week before. Inquiring minds want to know, so I asked why. She explained that it takes her awhile to settle in.

At some point during all of this levity, Hubby decided to head off to the library to get a book. As he disappeared from sight Ann remarked how she's surprised at the number of single men on board who had wanted to chat with her. I wonder could it be the boobies or her charm.

Ann told us she started her trip by flying from California to Paris alone and staying in a hotel. How brave! Then she took a train to Venice and stayed several weeks before boarding the ship. What a fascinating woman!

We notice a woman with her back to us was taking her arms out of her bathing suit. She slipped on a tee shirt and dropped her suit to her waist. We're staring as she sat down, facing us, put a beach towel over her lap as she wiggled out of her suit. Her butt's now on the cold marble. Could that be to cool off her too hot bottom? Calmly she dropped the suit and pulled up Capri pants. She picked up the suit and strolled away.

We can't hold back our laughter. "People ask me what I like about cruises, howls Ann. "I tell them you see all kinds of wonderful, exciting and wild things." I tell her I like cruises because I think I'm just normal looking, but after looking at others on the cruise ship, I think I look damned good.

Too bad Hubby missed out.

Venice—it's so classic and lovely. All of the streets in one direction are canals. In order to walk along the other streets you have to walk up steps, then cross the canal bridge, go down more steps, walk a block, and do it all over again. If you see the movie "The Tourist," you'll understand. It was difficult with "the hip". We saw Venice with our family guides, T.J. and R.R. My son was very sweet letting me hold onto his arm as we went up and down. Visiting Venice twenty years ago would have been more fun. It was magnificent, nevertheless.

We flew to Dusseldorf, Germany, rented a car, dropped off our luggage and drove to Cologne. Getting lost several times allowed us to see a lot of the lush green countryside and more of Cologne than we planned. We were on our way to see the famous Cologne Catholic Cathedral. It was fabulous! The church was spared during World War II, when all of the buildings around it were bombed. We joined other tourist in the back of the cathedral. A Mass was in progress and the music was awesome.

We found a good German restaurant and enjoyed "people watching." Europeans make going out to eat in the evening a big deal. They take their time enjoying family and friends. Probably it's an experience that doesn't happen often due to the expense.

After getting lost again we arrived at the hotel, ready to rest, but not ready for our long flight. On the way home Hubby and I couldn't sleep. We left in the morning and it was daylight all the way. Twelve hours later we arrived in Miami mid-afternoon. A teething toddler liked crying and wasn't having fun either.

I got to talking to a woman who was born and raised in Paris. Now she lived in Munich, Germany, with her cute husband and pre-teen and teenage sons. They were going to Florida on a vacation. I let her read a chapter of my book which led her to give me her email so she can get my book. Cool!

I loved a lot about our trip, but unfortunately, I'm not a good traveler. Not sure if I'll go again. If we were to go again, we would want to take a repositioning cruise. This is when the cruise ships reposition themselves for summer European cruises. A lot of them go to the Mediterranean. This allows people to adjust to the time changes and arrive rested. Too bad they got rid of the planes that made it from N.Y. to Paris in three hours.

It was interesting going back to Germany after almost thirty years. Getting lost, we noticed that signs would be in German with English written underneath. The bombed out buildings were all gone now.

Thirty years ago T.J. was stationed at Ramstein Air Force Base in mid-Germany. He took us all over Southern Germany and out of Paris during rush hour, which was very hectic, with lots of streets coming into the big five lane round-about. We went to museums, restaurants and even a large department store in Paris. Interesting to me was the large 6'x 9' area that had Dr. Scholl's products. (Hey Girlie, wear high heels long enough and it will cause foot problems. How many old ladies do you see wearing high heels?) We only encountered two rude people there at that time. No rude French since.

From Paris we drove South through the wine country. We stopped in a darling little village for lunch.

T.J. is an amazing guy. With just his High School French (okay, and charm) he was able to be understood. He learned enough Spanish to get by, but how he learned German was and is a mystery. When he was a child he had to go to speech therapy for a hearing discrimination problem. His parents both have the same challenge.

We continued southwest over the French Alps to Coasta de Sol in Spain. We spent a few days enjoying the sites and the company of very friendly people. We returned to T.J.'s apartment and took time to see Munich. What fun those German beer gardens were, even if you don't drink beer. We spent a night at the military base. It had been a wonderful trip.

The differences in thirty years were rather surprising. Hubby and I noticed the following: Europe seems to be very prosperous, with more consumer items available. Seldom did we see empty stores. There seemed to be a lot more young and middle aged people. Europeans are much more fit than Americans. This age group looks like Americans—lots of jeans. More Europeans speak English and are very helpful and seem friendlier. We also found travel easier because most countries now use the Euro. Before we had to go into a bank to exchange currency in each country. No bank machines thirty years ago. The big, wonderful change was no more stopping at every border to show uniformed military police our passports. This was unpleasant as these guys did not joke around. Before stamping, they would take all passports, and then look in the car to identify you by photo. There always seemed to be lines of vehicles waiting. Since most European countries are small, it would be like stopping at each of our state lines.

We noticed that the individual countries don't seem to be as individual as thirty years ago. I loved it. If it weren't such a pain to get there and cost so much, I would want to go there more often. Hey, they have fun, cute waiters, great food, and beautiful sites-what else do you want? Texas?? That's a fun place too. Where else can you get on a steer and have your photo made?

Seriously . . . . travel before you're too old. You'll enjoy it more. And hold on to your panties and have fun.

54

Fun with Southerners

Southerners can be tender and kind, kind, kind. What I love most is their seemingly proper demeanor and yet when you get to know them, you often find they have a wicked, wonderful bad ass sense of humor. They seem to have a twisted view of life that I love.

Most of the fun in this book has happened in the South where I have lived most of my life. I met my first Southerners at Mary Washington College in Fredericksburg, Virginia. Girls from Southern states not only talked differently, but they usually looked at life in a humorous way. My roommate was from Montgomery, Alabama. You can't get more Southern than that, can you?

Southern girls are taught to be nice. Sometimes they take great pride in being nicer, cuter, and better at anything than you. If they love you they are your best sister friend. Southerners use subtle inflections when slamming someone often unrealized by the person insulted. If you do them wrong—watch out.

Southerners tend to speak and move more slowly, but not mentally. Their soft lilting language is made up of words that are a bit different. A Southerner may say they went to see Joe when he died. Kind of like meeting him instead of viewing him.

A few years ago Ludlow Porch, an Atlanta radio celebrity said, "Naked means no clothes, but Nekkid means no clothes and up to no good."

Studies show people who live in Southern climates are more outgoing and optimistic. I have found this true in our country and in Europe.

Southern boys usually have much better manners. They are afraid their mama will KILL them if they don't behave properly.

You might say-	Southerners usually say-
Hi	Hey
Sweetie	Sugah
Crazy Acting	Hissy Fit
Cockroach	Water bug
Country bumpkins	Redneck
Grandpa	Paw paw
Underwear	Unmentionables
A cute guy	Just the cutest thing
Poor guy	Bless his heart
Awful	Pitiful
Bringing up	Raising
No No	Ma'am
Baby	Precious baby
Potatoes	Taters
Babe	Southern Belle
Pop or Soda	Coke
Picking at	Nit Pickin'
For Sure	Bet your britches
Take	Carry
Turn off	Cut off-as in cut off the water
Going to the mall	Fixin' to go to the mall
Yes	Yes ma'am

Now you can reread Faulkner or Celia Rivenbark (my favorite best friend I haven't met yet) and better understand what they are saying.

A Southern friend says, "There is nothing like an 80-year old Southern woman with a great sense of wit, who can take you out at the knees and you don't even know you hit the porch." I know <u>exactly</u> what she means. My sweet looking friend Faye, from North Carolina, at 80, verbally nearly knocked me down as she asked why I always ate the same foods. I told her about my food allergies. She says, "With all you have wrong with you Emily—your mama should have pinched your head off when you were born." Is that just too funny? Southern writers seem to develop humorous interesting characters that I love. Among my favorites are Mary Kay Andrews, Hissy Fit; Jill Conner Browne, Sweet Potato Queen's Book of Love; Fannie Flagg, who wrote Fried Green Tomatoes; Dorothea Benton Frank, Pawleys Island; Kathy Patrick, The Pulpwood Queen's Tiara-Wearing, Book-Sharing Guide to Life; Celia Rivenbark, You Can't Drink All Day If You Don't Start in the Morning; Anne Rivers Siddons, Kings Oak; Haywood Smith, Queen Bee of Mimosa Branch; and Rebecca Wells author of Divine Secrets of the YA-YA Sisterhood.

One of my very favorite books is It's a Chick Thing, edited by Ame Mahler Beanland, Emily Miles Terry and Jill Conner Browne. This is a collection of stories of very funny girlfriends having way too much fun.

Let me know if you enjoyed reading this book and want to be emailed when my new book, Hold On To Your Panties and Decorate Too is published which contains lots of great decorating hints and more funny stories.

However, Sweet Young Things, don't expect a speedy reply. I'm working on getting stuff done for the next book, playing bridge, painting, reading, traveling and generally raising hell. Expect less?

Terrific Tributes

Thank you Hubby for your loving support! Your wit keeps me going, your intelligence and calm personality inspire me. Your strength in the face of trauma and drama makes me want to be like you. As long as you feed us and we keep laughing, Diva THE Dalmatian and I will keep you. You lucky guy!

Tributes go also to my loving, fun family, especially Justine for your writing advice.

Kissy, Kissy, Kissups!

Oh poo—this is the hardest part for me to write as I don't want to leave anyone out.

Without the aid, kindness and encouragement of many people, this book would not be a reality. You know who you are, and are not!

Magnificent Maggie DeVries, the leader of our local Florida writing group, coach and friend. You have been a real gem. (Like your book store "Books Plus".) Your humor, advice and knowledgeable assistance has been wonderful.

Awesome artists, Deb Milbrath and Pat Mennenger, I am jealous of your talents and appreciate you both. You made the front and back covers stand out. Bravo!

Kind Karen Johnson who typed and retyped the manuscript again, again and again. Your 1000 watt smile and sense of humor kept me going. Thank you!

Lovely Lucy Herring, your sweet caring kindness and editing have kept me from "writer's insanity". You stepped in when I needed you most. Thank you so much!

My sweet, sassy sister, your support and reading suggestions have been awesome! I am very glad I prayed for a little sister. You are very special to me!

Judylicious Stroup, head of my research department and constant cheerleader, you have been terrific! I thank you for your timely advice and wildly funny humor.

Merry Mother Marie Straub, you were the voice of reason to someone we know, who wasn't always reasonable—me. Thank you for all you have done, girlfriend deluxe.

Charming Carlynne Easterwood, my young, "Annie Air Force Reserve" friend, thank you for being my number one fan! Could you be my secret love child?

Brilliant Brett Carter, restaurant owner, interior designer, singer etc. Thanks for your loving support, kindness and humor.

Applause, applause, applause goes to friends who have been supportive in various groups that I have been or am currently involved in as a member:

- The Florida Writers (state and local)
- Curves
- TOPS in Florida and North Carolina
- Florida Newcomers bridge and book groups
- North Carolina Senior Bridge group
- The Dalmatian Club of America
- The Greater Atlanta Dalmatian Club
- The Central Florida Dalmatian Club

Accolades go to the fun people in the book, as well as those who helped by reading, giving advice, doing additional typing and by their wonderful support. They are Viv Martin, Arva Butler, Beth Mansbridge, Mary Jane Elsworth, Merry Carol Houchard, Betty Guerrero, Chuck Rogers, Joy Nichels Wilson, Jo Brayshaw, Linda Schuller Bradley, Terri Kiker, Cheryl and Buddy Coe, Judy Clark, Joni Shoup and Julia Soukup (friend and web site designer), Loretta Clark, Sandy Anderson, Betty Sutton, Margie Finnigan and Gerda Shreve. Ross Gass, Jane Allison, Georgia Marshat, Dee Holland, Helene Henline, Peggy Lawhorne, Jackie Wesley, Brett Carter, Melody Adams and Nore Pope.

If I left anyone out, bless your heart, deal with it, I didn't do it on purpose.

If you find errors, Bless your heart, I can't control everyone and everything.

If you have funny decorating stories or anything GOOD to say, e-mail me at emilyjoannehoover@gmail.com. Don't expect an answer as I will be out "having fun with my panties on" or writing.

God bless you for buying this book and for being you.

Fun and Funny Excerpts From "Hold On To Your Panties and Have Fun" By Emily Joanne Hoover

This book doesn't contain anything perishable, liquid, or flammable. It does contain interesting, somewhat racy and shocking life stories that will have you LAUGHING OUT LOUD as you gain insight into your own life. In order to understand this book you may need to know how family and friends describe me.

"Funny" By a lot of people. Hey, better than funny looking.

"Life of the party" Maybe.

"Amusing" Could it be?

"Hot Lips" High school and college friends who tease me about playing the trumpet and the mellophone.

"Mischievous" You think?

"Inspirational" Really?

"Hot Foot" Isn't that what the fast lane is for? After all, being called "Hot Foot" and "Hot Lips" is the closest I have gotten to being called "A Hottie."

"Bad" I just try to make life around me as interesting and fun as possible.

Some women might be horrified to be called bad. Since I am really good at being bad, I consider it an honor.

- People seldom talk about underwear. I love to have fun with underwear. Maybe not the kind of fun you are thinking of. Last summer while at Walmart, my eye happens to catch sight of tiger print bikini panties. They were on sale for $3.00! Who of my many girlfriends could I have the most fun sending these to? Soon I am grinning thinking of my new adorable daughter-in-law and Viv, my 85 year old red-headed friend who acts 45, and is starting to date a younger guy. Both of these gals share my "wicked bad ass" sense of humor. I have to tell "the check out lady," I plan to send the card with the panties that says, "Put a tiger in your tank girlfriend-grrr." She giggles and I laugh all the way home.

I tell Hubby my plan and he grins. Soon I was on my way to the post office. The guy there recognizes me. He asks me if I have anything liquid, perishable, flammable, etc. I say, "No, they are just "tiger panties." His blush made my day! The very next day I see Viv at bridge. She comes over, grinning and thanks me for the panties. I say, " What panties?" "You know damn well what panties. None of my other friends would do that!"

I said "Really? What a pity," as I grin. She went on to say they "fit perfectly." I love making people happy.

- One when our oldest son was about 11 we were eating dinner and discussing the planned breeding of our first Champion Dalmatian. I said, "Can you believe that I was the only one in my family that was planned?" Quick on the draw, S.C. said, "Gee, Mom to look at you, no one would believe you were planned." I do so love it when someone "gets me" good.

- One day a pal of T.J.'s went with us to the Atlanta show, which was held not far from home. While I was chatting with a friend, T.J. took one of the dogs to the van. He returned to tell me we had to stay for Best in Show. He said he overheard that several of the professional handlers had gone together to hire a streaker, who would be appearing during Best in Show. The boys were excited. (They were about 12 at the time.) Hey, they might see a naked woman! I seriously doubted that something like that would happen. The show chairman was an older gal who was quite dignified, as was the judge. I told the boys this and decided to stay anyway, since it would soon be time for Best in Show, which is always exciting.

Well, it was more exciting than I ever expected. The judge moved the dogs around the ring. Just before he was to go over the first dog, a young gal (20-30 years old) in a raincoat and a wide-brimmed hat, appeared at ringside. She quickly removed the coat and ran diagonally across the ring in green knee socks- minus shoes and clothes. About halfway across the ring she took off her hat and let her long hair fall out. Everyone laughed as she got red. She quickly disappeared, and the judging continued. That was the last time T.J.'s little friend went with us. His mom didn't speak to me again. I found out the handlers were "fun guys" I knew.

- As Hubby and I were finishing the building of our Florida home, I checked daily to see how things were coming along. One day I was up in the bonus room talking with the building contractor. Up the stairs came an adorable 30-somthing electrician. He was tall, dark hair, great big blue eyes, and a damn fine muscled body. (Ok, I had to say it so you'd get the picture.) I was standing about three feet from the stairs when he appeared. I said to him, "Hi, I'm Emily." To the contractor I said, "You didn't tell me he was so handsome." The electrician blushed, grinned, tripped and fell about three feet from me. I said, "I've waited all my life for a guy to fall at my feet." Unfortunately, I haven't seen him since. Fifteen years, but who's counting?

- A few years ago Ludlow Porch, an Atlanta radio celebrity said, "Naked means no clothes, but Nekkid means no clothes and up to no good."

  A Southern friend says, "There is nothing like an 80-year old Southern woman with a great sense of wit, who can take you out at the knees and you don't even know you hit the porch." I know exactly what she means. My sweet looking friend Faye, from North Carolina, at 80, verbally nearly knocked me down as she asked why I always ate the same foods. I told her about my food allergies. She says, "With all you have wrong with you Emily—your mama should have pinched your head off when you were born." Is that just too funny?

  FOR MORE FUN STORIES BUY THIS BOOK, OK?

Discussion Questions

1. What is your favorite chapter? Why?
2. Did you think the title and cover were appropriate? Why?
3. Did you learn anything from this book?
4. What made you laugh out loud?
5. Which of the author's best friends would you like to get to know?
6. Would you like to hang out with the author?
7. How do you think you may be changing as the years go by?
8. Which part of the book do you think was the most fun?
9. What is your idea of FUN?